THE
EMPTY DESK
SURVIVAL GUIDE

FOR WOMEN ON THE VERGE OF
RETIREMENT OR ENCORE CAREERS

BARBARA BANNON
ARLENE CHEMERS
MARYLOVE THRALLS

ISBN: 1467963895
ISBN 13: 9781467963893

Library of Congress Control Number: 2011961543
CreateSpace, North Charleston, SC

CONTENTS

PREFACE

Welcome!

You are entering uncharted territory. You have not ventured down this path before, and the terrain can be unfamiliar and unforgiving. Any wise adventurer, like you, knows that for the most successful – and least-perilous journey, a survival guide is not simply a "great beach read." We've assembled a thoughtful survival kit based on experience and research you simply must not leave without.

You can – and should leave behind the outdated "inspirational" calendars, the piles of business cards old enough not to have website and e-mail information, the baggies stuffed with assorted thicknesses and colors of ballpoint pens you're not even sure are still usable, the "gift" coffee mugs attractively sporting advertisers' logos, congealed rubber bands and those broken-off clusters of staples you've never tried to stuff back in your stapler but felt guilty about tossing into the trash. Discard all the unmatched envelopes and cards. The scraps of paper with things you were supposed to remember to do but didn't. The plaques for participating in local charities are commendable, but not portable – remember you want to survive this expedition! You will probably be carrying around enough personal/emotional baggage that the less you are encumbered with the flotsam and jetsam of your career, the better off you will be, and the more likely to survive "The Empty Desk Syndrome."

Our survival kit is very compact and fits neatly into your pocket, backpack, laptop, Kindle, or iPad, so we highly recommend you keep it handy for those times when the road ahead is obscured or when you seem to have traveled the same path over and over again, or when "the road less traveled" looks way too foreboding.

Your "Empty Desk Survival Guide" is a real bargain -- and we all love a great bargain - because it comes with a team of traveling companions -- experienced guides who've confronted many of the pitfalls that could highjack your self-confidence, sabotage your expectations, and put you at risk for a difficult transition from the person you once were to the person you will become. They will be by your side every step of the way.

Ready to go? Your future is waiting. Come, meet your fellow travelers...

INTRODUCTION

Feminist icon Betty Friedan had her finger on the sensitive pulse emanating from the "retirement paradox" the feminist movement created. She observed that in a society in which prestige and power were equated to occupational status and income, the women who now achieve this "personhood" equally with men also face similar challenges as their male counterparts when approaching retirement and the perceived loss of prestige and power. But how these challenges are met and overcome are as different as the gender of the prospective retirees.

"The Empty Desk Survival Guide" was conceived and written by women, for women, as a resource for those coming to terms with the emotional impact of leaving the corporate board room, the corner office, the partnership, the podium or desk that long served as their personal "command central."

It's one thing to eagerly anticipate the final day at a job that has, at most, been something merely tolerated for years, or a place of business that has failed to nurture one's creativity, leadership, or camaraderie. But it is a far different story when one must reluctantly hang up the gavel, turn over the files and the corporate credit card, or terminate a professional position that has been both defining and rewarding on many levels.

How does the successful career woman "let go" of all that? Or does she?

"The Empty Desk..." is a practical guide designed to assist that very Baby Boomer Super Woman navigate through this difficult, often unexamined process. The good news is that there are women willing to share their stories to light the way, and step-by-step proven-successful evaluation tools to steer the reader toward a rewarding post-career resolution based on her own unique situation.

CO-AUTHOR'S INSIGHTS AND REFLECTIONS:

Of the three of us, I am the oldest and have been officially retired for 6 years so I can easily relate to many of the stories of the women we interviewed. All of these women experienced growing up during the late forties and fifties with similar childhood experiences and programming on being a "woman," which was based on the ideal image of the fifties mother.

I was very impressed with the energy, innovativeness and creativity of the women we interviewed whose lives turned out to be very different than their mothers' lives. I can also relate to them as part of the first generation of women who moved into the male dominated working world with personal experiences in many different business environments.

I have worked for over twenty-five years in the public and private sectors and have also owned my own coaching and training company. I have also been trained as a professional coach and am a certified retirement coach. Therefore, I was certain that I would successfully transition to this next phase of my life, "retirement." Intellectually, I knew what to consider, how to plan and how to deal with the changes, challenges, losses and how to avoid common pitfalls.

I transitioned slowly by accepting a part-time coaching and training position at a career development company. Working on a consulting basis allowed me to travel with my husband for several years, volunteering at national and state parks. We had a wonderful taste of one type of retirement lifestyle and loved it.

Currently, we are adjusting to a less fluid lifestyle and I am beginning to understand personally and emotionally, the adjustments required by the retiree as time goes by. I have discovered that there is not just a single retirement transition time, although leaving work feels like the big one at the time. Retirement life will require continual transitioning. Therefore, the reader will be able to turn to the exercises we present in this book as they continually assess the three questions of retirement life:

WHO AM I NOW? WHAT DO I WANT? HOW DO I GET THERE?

-Arlene Chemers

The process of interviewing, writing and reading these women's stories was quite an interesting "task." But when I finally got off "task" and began to let myself reflect and savor the stories and experiences these women presented, it took me on quite a trip. I don't know for sure if anyone else can relate to this but there have been times in my life when the things going on around me were so intense I, not always intentionally, minimized the emotion and impact I'd allow the event or experience to have on me.

I finally allowed myself to feel and think about the twists and turns these women's lives took and the effects it had on them, and the effect it had on me because I realized I had shared many of these experiences, both the good and not so good. Of course I can now be philosophical about all the experiences I've had and accepting that it made me the person I am today, although at times I can feel unhappy about that outcome, but still accepting.

Also in this, my time of reflecting, I realize more than ever that as part of this rather large group of women we have a long way to go and lots more potential adventures ahead. Much luck to my co-writers and all the other women who find themselves on this journey!

- **Barbara Bannon**

The process of creating this book was more of a learning experience for me than I ever anticipated -- and on more than one level! My appreciation of, and admiration for, my co-authors has deepened and been enriched beyond measure. I am grateful for their wisdom and insight – illuminated via Skype (this is after all, the electronic age) as we worked through revision after revision until we were all satisfied that we had something that would really answer a need and be useful to others.

The gift of the stories of the women I interviewed was received most humbly. How generous they have been to share their lives with us, and how much we can all learn from each other's experiences is amazing. Finding myself in their midst and wrangling with similar issues and concerns about the future, I take strength in their steadfastness and belief that this journey will be worth taking.

Rather than facing the future with fear, we must value all the days of our lives as precious and not to be squandered. If there's anything our readers take away from this book, my hope is, that it is that one truth.

- **Marylove Thralls**

PART ONE

READY! AIM! FIRED!
WHEN LAYOFFS AND LIFE
INTERRUPT THE BEST LAID PLANS

No matter how carefully we plan ahead, even allowing for unforeseen contingencies, situations arise that we are forced to deal with in the best way we can at the time. But when our "survival skills" come up short and our coping mechanisms fail, how can we overcome serious setbacks to our vision for the future? The women you will meet in this section of your Survival Guide met some serious challenges with both some common feelings, and some not-so common responses as: regret, shock, anger, pluck and imagination. We can all learn from their stories.

Our hope, in sharing these stories, is that they provide something of value for you, whether it be insight, hope, comfort or just the knowledge that you aren't alone in this adventure. As you read along, you might find the answer to questions you wouldn't have known you needed to ask. To assist you we've provided some processing questions at the end of each story to help you formulate your own direction.

Earlier Than Planned or Not Quite Ready:

Sometimes life doesn't go as planned and that can certainly be the case these days with regard to the changing workplace. Additionally, as one prepares for any transformational change in life, like retirement, a critical part of that process is the phase of mulling it over, imagining, assessing, etc., and you'll be reading a story about one interviewee who is doing just that. In this section you'll meet women whose stories may have similarities to the circumstances in which you find or have found yourself.

The Accidental Traveler

While she had been careful about saving for the future, Barbara had not planned for the day when she was "offered" a choice to either resign immediately or take a serious reduction in pay and responsibilities! After 31 years with the same Fortune 500 industry leader, it was inconceivable to her that this was happening. After all, she had accepted more complex projects and had greater autonomy than ever before in her career. She had traveled to countries where governments were in chaos and charged with helping these troubled industry hubs streamline their operations. Surely, she had become indispensable within their hi-tech systems division, hadn't she?

As Barbara came to learn unexpectedly, as with almost any American corporation in the twenty-first century, *every* employee ultimately is expendable. Hopefully for most of our readers, retirement will be a planned process and the timing something each one has some control over. For Barbara, this was not the case, obviously. Although she had built up a sufficient nest egg through solid investments and by living well within her means, she was suddenly confronted with unemployment – albeit under the cushion of a "golden parachute."

After assessing the ramifications of the offer from the company with a long-time financial advisor, Barbara was able to take a deep breath and attempt to get her bearings. The company's settlement would not leave her "well off" but she would be comfortable for a very long time, as long as she kept to a budget and continued to live modestly and stayed healthy.

More than the loss of income, the most serious blow however, was to her self-esteem. The idea of no longer being necessary to the organization to which she gave far more of herself than her position warranted, was difficult to accept: "Prior to retirement I had this attitude that I just *had* to be at work – in hindsight, I spent way too much time there – being a good employee, getting everything done. I often put work ahead of friends and family." Despite situations when Barbara would have to report to someone who was abusive, or find herself under too much stress without adequate compensation for "going the extra mile," she had made up her mind to "stick it out" until she was at least 60. After all, she was doing work that essentially gave her satisfaction, pushed her intellectually and was personally rewarding.

The package the company offered would be adequate, especially with the possibility of working as an outside consultant for the company on occasion when her expertise was needed. But that was in 2000 when the economy began to decline, and after 9/11, this particular industry spiraled out of control, and any hopes of augmenting her retirement income through consulting there were dashed.

Her initial loss of self-esteem was tempered during the early phase of her surprise retirement, because in the sudden economic downturn, she was sharply aware of many, many others – and even a few close colleagues – going through a similar situation. "I have never had an issue of identity and have been comfortable in my own skin," she notes, and in fact, "I ultimately became a role model for some of my friends – retire early and have fun while you still can."

But it took her almost a year to get over the feelings she had after losing her job. "I'd wake up some nights with the same thoughts running through my head. I didn't expect that!" Barbara eventually was able to let go of the shock and disappointment of being terminated. She let go of the past to make room for the future. And to her, the future was bright! Because of her benefits package she could continue to indulge in her love for travel indefinitely.

But life interrupted her plans once again.

"Some things happen for a reason," Barbara says philosophically. Her mother became seriously ill, suffering a series of strokes, ultimately having to be moved into an assisted living facility. Her home would have to be sold, and her belongings distributed among family members or sold, a financial plan made, a healthcare advocate found, and other time-consuming tasks had to be handled. Because she did not have to juggle a job and travel half-way across the country a multitude of times in response to her mother's illness, Barbara was able to be with her mother throughout the final months of her life, when her mother needed her the most. She was later available to be a caregiver to a beloved cousin before she died of cancer. "I could not have done all that and continued working in the job I had, so in hindsight, it was a fortunate thing."

Barbara now travels and visits friends she has made all over the world, and continues to enjoy meeting new people and learning about other cultures. She supports a rural school in China, and visits the school every couple of years. She most recently completed a pilgrimage in Spain that is part of a centuries-old tradition there. Over the years of travel she has honed her photographic skills and chronicled her adventures. Perhaps when she has time a travel memoir might be part of her future endeavors. "I have time to try new things, like writing and research, and if I ever get bored or depressed, I have only myself to blame – and I find new things to do very fast. I don't know what will happen if/when my health does not allow me to be a gypsy, but until then, I am going to continue to do whatever strikes me."

One of the best things in her view about retirement is being able to turn off the alarm clock and not have to face rush hour traffic. While it does take time to establish a new rhythm, Barbara is more than happy not to feel the same stressors as people she knows who are still struggling in the corporate world and hating their jobs: "Being on this side of it makes you really appreciate getting out. Sometimes I do get to feeling that I am wasting time or not doing anything mean- ingful – but usually that leaves very fast. It doesn't take me long to find something else to do that is interesting and fulfilling – whether it be gardening, reading or finding someplace else to explore. I would not take a job like the one I had for anything at this point in my life!"

One new addition to her lifestyle is educational consulting work, which has evolved into some joint publishing. Barbara often finds her- self eagerly finishing assignments. This work helps supplement her monthly retirement income (including a 401K and IRA) along with Social Security which she applied for at age 62. While the amount she receives is less than if she had waited until 66, she now has more of a financial cushion. She still watches her expenses but in the last year has been able to buy a new car, have work done on her house, and travel wherever and whenever she likes. "I don't feel like I am deny- ing myself at all. After the first few years, when I was getting a han- dle on life without a job, I can now be less concerned about making it."

But Barbara does have some advice for those contemplating not working at all or very little, post-retirement. The first thing she did was to look at all her expenses and put together a basic budget she thought she could live on. She doesn't have cable television or long distance calling on her phone. (The cell phone she uses is "pay as you go" and she uses a calling card for long distance.) She cooks her own meals at home as much as possible – more nutritious and less expensive, and uses the library rather than buying the latest $25 hardback book. "Since I now have more time to read, this could be an expensive habit," she notes with amusement.

Barbara engaged a financial analyst and human resource expert to help her sort through different options, especially with regard to taking retirement and social security early or delaying for a higher payout, and what the break-even time-frames would be. She decided to take both right away: "Too many people are not getting to the break-even years, "she said. "I am the only person I can turn to if I get into financial trouble, so I have no other fall-back plan. But then again, I don't have to take care of anyone other than myself. Once you know what your financial issues are, then you can put together a plan to have fun – travel or whatever, and still feel you will be safe."

Her attitude is a big departure from the attitude of her mother's generation – those men and women who were a product of the Great Depression and worried continually about running out of money. When her mother was ill, it took a social worker a long time to convince her that the rainy day she had been saving for all her life was now.

Yet Barbara now worries about her nephews and the younger generation for whom the prospect of retirement planning and government support appears to be on shaky ground, coupled with "gen-x" attitudes about spending now while you have it. "They buy much fancier clothes, and cars and houses, but they are enjoying life now, while they are young and most able to. Lots to be said in favor of that! Who knows what tomorrow will bring? When I first got out of school, retirement was the furthest thing from my mind, but I think I successfully made the transition."

For our Accidental Tourist, retirement is "more like the start of life than what some see as an end of life." That's good news, isn't it!

SURVIVAL QUESTIONS:

1. How do you think you would have handled this situation?
2. What did you appreciate most about how Barbara handled her termination?
3. What stood out most in Barbara's story for you?
4. What did you find most valuable?
5. What wisdom can you apply to your situation?

OUR OBSERVATIONS:

- Her forced retirement ended the illusion of being indispensible.
- Barbara saved, sought financial consulting, and redefined a budget looking at need versus want.
- If you experience an initial loss of identity and self esteem – don't stay there! Barbara didn't stay there, and now does educational consulting using her transferrable skills.
- Personal health issues came as a surprise: she is concerned about her future health and her ability to keep on doing the same, like we all are.
- Like Barbara, keep redefining who you are.
- Time became available for Barbara for caregiving, to experience loss, and enjoy the freedom to respond to relationship needs and desires.
- Try to avoid limiting thoughts with regard to what you can do or try.
- Learn to enjoy the small stuff in life: i.e. Not having to get up to the alarm, noticing what is around you.
- Retirement is another transition in life: we're just more conscious of it than we were of the other transitions.

- Women who are corporate contributors tend to have more trouble with identity than women who have a stand-alone profession, (i.e. an occupation versus a job title).

- Barbara has built a world-wide support network and relies on it.

- The win-win -- Barbara has time to travel all she wants, and uses her free time for philanthropy, volunteering in local performing arts venues, and pursuing her hobbies in writing and photography.

THE ALCHEMIST

"When life gives you lemons, you turn it into lemonade." Throughout Judy's life, she has had the uncanny ability to transform adversity into golden opportunities to learn and grow. Even the most recent and life-threatening detour from a thoroughly enjoyable position in academia led Judy down a path to a new career she never dreamt would become her life's most significant work. But she saw potential for growth that only a true visionary would notice through the clouds of fear and pain.

Coming from a rural town in the Southwest, she was always eager to learn from everything around her. Perhaps her mother's "lady friends" cultivated her life-long interest in knitting, weaving and quilting, and the crop dusters droning like lazy bees overhead instilled in her a passion to soar above the fields. An only child, she was an avid reader and it was no surprise that she would earn a masters degree in Library Science. But it *was* remarkable that she not only learned how to fly, but she did it so well she became a flight instructor and one of the first women ever to sell aviation training equipment.

Deceptively demure in a "Mary Engelbreit" way, her sparkling blue eyes give the first indication of an inquisitive nature and steely determination to make the most of life. In addition to Library Science, Judy also acquired an advanced degree in Counseling and Psychological Services that would serve a natural desire to nurture and guide others. She melded both degrees in a nearly twenty-year stint within the public library system until she became irresistibly drawn to the concept of travel and teaching. So she moved to the east coast to study and train to be an instructor in ESL (English as a Second Language).

Her father's illness and death interrupted this plan, so Judy took a job with a large international corporation as a training and development manager to be able to spend more time back home with her mother. The company provided a flexible schedule and she was able to give comfort and support for her mom, and later, to oversee her care to the extent that her mother was able to stay in the family home until she, too, passed away. But first and foremost, this position also offered Judy the opportunity to make use of her counseling skills, coaching team leaders and problem-solving personnel issues.

When a downturn in the economy resulted in a departmental reorganization, Judy and the HR staff were required to do the same amount of work with fewer people, which many of us can no doubt relate to. Seeing the writing on the wall, Judy networked like mad and when she lost her job officially, soon had another position lined up that would tap into her natural bent toward helping others. "I detoured through to career counseling as a segue to coaching but had never been involved in academia before. It felt at first like an interim move, but I quickly grew very fond of the students and staff. Helping students think about their futures was so rewarding."

With the final days of her mother's life, Judy came into intimate contact with the hospice movement. True to her fashion, she learned all she could about hospice care and joined a bereavement writing group, which helped her personally so much that she became a volunteer. "I wasn't ready to give up the financial security of my full-time job," Judy admitted, but she was so drawn to hospice work that she acquired certification in Thanatology through the Association for Death Education and Counseling.

Judy was not prepared however, for the next detour along her path.

While she was still working at the college, she received the kind of news everyone dreads: she was diagnosed with a rare form of cancer. Her inquisitive nature rose to the challenge, and with her life partner Alan, the internet was mined for every possible link to the causation and available remedies for this virulent form of the disease. She identified a facility she believed would best suit her needs and in fact, the Dana Farber Institute proved to be worthy of her trust.

Judy's treatment was intense. She had to focus all of her energy on surviving the chemical treatments that sapped her strength and compromised her immune system. As a consummate networker, her friends found they could count on her for thorough updates via lengthy and often amusing e-mail accounts of her ups and downs throughout the process of surgery, recovery and ultimate healing and celebration.

Typical of Judy, the "time off" was not entirely about rest and recuperation. She did a lot of soul searching and determined that she wanted to continue to help people regardless of her situation. "As you yourself are growing older, you develop your own philosophy about life that is deeper and more outward-looking: What can I do to make an impact on the world I live in."

Today, she is "semi-retired," working part-time as a bereavement coordinator for a hospice program in the Massachusetts area. She provides grief education and support to bereaved hospice family and community members, and works closely with social workers and chaplains to ensure those experiencing anticipatory grief have a safe place to express their feelings.

While she was in recovery from the chemotherapy, and not yet able to assume the position with the hospice program, Judy received a newsletter from a fiber arts organization called WARP. They were in need of an Administrative Coordinator. She jumped at the opportunity to get involved – right from her perch on the couch. "This is something I can do at home," she thought, eager to turn her recovery period into something productive. The organization operates a networking website for weavers and fiber artists around the world and the position would require only 25 hours a month. She could help countless women in far-off third world countries find a voice and a living wage for their laborious artistry.

The anniversary of her recovery was celebrated with a trip to the Greek Islands with Alan. Those golden sunsets across the caldera off Santorini, seemed a fitting reward for a long journey with many detours that led Judy to her true life's work.

SURVIVAL QUESTIONS:

1. What did you appreciate most about Judy's story?
2. Can you imagine yourself doing anything like this?
3. Which of Judy's ideas most appeal to you?

OUR OBSERVATIONS:

- Judy has grit, which is demonstrated throughout her entire life and into retirement. It appears that she arises to any occasion and challenge with which she is presented.

- She never gives up and makes the very best of each situation. She conquers each challenge with learning (researching) and then doing.

- She is flexible and has the ability to adapt.

- She is a life-long learner. (hand crafts, flying, teaching, training, coaching, administrative coordinator to hospice work).

- She is proactive, plans and prepares ahead for upcoming transitions and changes.

- She combines all of her strengths together at each stage of her life to create something new. (i.e. ESL/travel; position as Administrative Coordinator, hospice, pursuing new certifications), hence, the title "Alchemist" is very appropriate.

- She is a strong networker.

- She created the hospice position in semi-retirement understanding her need to nurture, coach, guide and counsel and her desire to impact the world and turn outward.

- Judy approached retirement or semi-retirement with the same strengths and orientation that she approached her earlier life.

NOTE (An update): Judy recently e-mailed her friends about her current status with regard to her cancer treatment. With her permission we share this with our readers:

"I would not advocate experiencing long distance care giving, death of parents, and cancer treatment as avenues to a greater understanding of self, but I can say they continue to help me learn more about what it takes to get what I came to life for and the self-awareness and self-care necessary to live my life to the fullest. And in the self-care department, friends, like all of you, are the most important ingredients. So thank you again for being there."

THE COMEBACK KID

Most of the people who know Bobbi would describe her as upbeat, positive, energetic, and very generous. Those descriptors are particularly surprising given the challenges and transitions with which she has been confronted in her life. When she faced retirement from her legal practice at the age of 51, it was not by choice but based on the necessity of having to care for her husband of one year, who was dying of cancer. She had cut her practice from full time to half time three years earlier to help care for her oldest daughter who had been diagnosed with a brain tumor, and died, one year after she lost her husband.

To say she was in a state of utter despair and loss is an understatement. It defies imagination to describe the emotional toll, just one of these losses might have, but the loss of a child and husband within a year of one another has got to be one of the most-supreme challenges one could ever face. How do you come back to "normal" life after going to such an emotional depth?

What a way to start a retirement! But after a year of numbness and with the help and support of friends, Bobbi began the process of facing her life not as it was, but as it would now be.

Bobbi found herself at 55, divorced, widowed, and retired. What was she to do with all this retirement time? Had she made any preparations? "Nothing, except save money! Retirement was forced on me and after being off for four years and being such an emotional wreck, as an attorney, I didn't feel I was in the place to help others with their issues." She said she didn't feel a loss of identity; she still identified herself as an attorney even though she wasn't practicing. Bobbi sensed that her interests before retirement helped keep her going because she continued those activities with a greater sense of freedom than she had felt before. She could now spend more time skiing, golfing, running, dancing, socializing with friends, reading, going to movies, dinner parties, charity events and traveling.

During the course of what turned out to be a four-year recovery period, she met and married an older (but very youthful) man who had been a tremendous help and support through the tragic loss of her child and subsequent grieving that followed. This relationship only lasted two years as a marriage, but will last a lifetime as a friendship. During this time she enjoyed a lot of traveling and leisure activities only to find she wasn't ready for a "jetsetter" lifestyle. She needed to find something worthwhile to do to help keep her feeling stimulated and involved.

Given all she had been through with her husband and daughter, Bobbi's greatest concern for the retirement years was a medical issue: "I had fears about losing my mental capacity. Lack of challenge is one of the reasons I got involved in a couple of, what turned out to be, pretty challenging, business ventures, in which I not only invested, but also helped manage on a day-to-day basis. That fear is also why I work on crosswords and number puzzles everyday, I don't want to lose my mental alertness, and I see that happening to some of my older friends." Additionally, she jokingly talked of saving medication for the time she thought her life should come to an end, and then more seriously discussed the "end-of-life" topic.

But the Comeback Kid is a born survivor! Her ability to take charge, confront and deal with whatever situation is put in her path was learned at a very early age. She and her sisters were sent to live with their grandmother in another state when she was only six. Bobbi was eleven when her grandmother fell seriously ill, so she and her sisters returned by train to Oklahoma, to live with their mother and stepfather. She became a top-seeded tennis player in the state and was invited to attend Oklahoma State University on a scholarship a full year before she completed high school. Her experience in college mistakenly lead her to believe she wasn't college material: she returned home, completed high school, and got married at 18.

Bobbi became a cosmetologist, put her husband through school and had a child in the four years she was married. Her husband was supposed to put her through school after he completed his education, but it didn't turn out that way. He got involved with another woman, and by age 22, Bobbi was a single mom and on her own. She was pretty frightened and depressed -- so depressed her friends decided they needed to take her to New Orleans for Mardi Gras. This turned out to be a turning point for Bobbi as well, she met a golf pro who talked her into moving in with him and for a short four months she experienced a life style she never knew existed. What she did know was that if she aspired to such a lifestyle for herself and her daughter she would have to get a different type of education, which is exactly what she did. Although the relationship ended abruptly, Bobbi knew now in what direction she was headed -- law school.

As fate would have it she then met the man who would be her husband for the next 24 years. He was also her teacher, mentor, a wonderful stepfather to her oldest daughter and the father of her younger daughter. He was a very highly regarded college professor and therapist, someone who understood Bobbi's capabilities and desire for further education. Though that marriage ultimately ended in divorce, it didn't end the respect and appreciation she had for this very wonderful man. While they were together, Bobbi completed both her undergraduate degree and her jurist doctorate.

Becoming a successful attorney certainly buoyed Bobbi's self-esteem, to the extent that even in retirement, any issues with her identity were negligible, as she continues to think of herself as an attorney, along with her many other roles i.e. grandmother, sister, community volunteer.

"I don't think I have any problems there, I know who I am. I've made a very good life for myself. My friends are very important to me -- I have lots of friends and they, in some respects, are more important than my family. Not that I'm not concerned or don't love my family, but they have lives of their own so I don't spend as much time with them as I do with my friends."

Bobbi's mother wasn't a particularly friendly person. It seems she didn't have many friends and was alone much of the time, which might help explain Bobbi's need for companionship.

"I've enjoyed every minute of the free time I have as a retired person." It's also understandable why she feels such a strong sense of freedom to enjoy her life now: She has faced some of life's most difficult changes and challenges and has always managed to rethink, adjust and thrive. She is, after all, the Comeback Kid.

SURVIVAL QUESTIONS:

1. What are your predominate thoughts/feelings about this story?

2. How do you think you would have handled situations similar to those Bobbi encountered?

3. What stood out most in Bobbi's story for you?

4. Could you relate any aspects of her story to your life?

OUR OBSERVATIONS:

- Bobbi had a difficult early life, confronted with challenges and the need to endure many transitions (life, educational, professional). She probably learned coping and survival skills early.

- Her sense of self must be very strong after surviving so much disruption and tragedy (losing both a husband and daughter). Possibly having been a strong athlete contributed.

- She established interests and hobbies which she continues to enjoy in retirement (i.e. skiing, golfing, running, socializing, reading, parties, dancing, charity work and travel).

- The sense of professional identity seems to be related to her profession as an "attorney" and not with a position or company.

- Bobbi discovered that she needs something "worthwhile" to do. This may emanate from a fear of losing mental capacity and fear of lack of challenge in her life. (This from a person that has been faced with more than her share of challenges!)

- She relies on her friends for support, more than her family. Understandable in light of how often "family" failed her.

- She manages to "rethink", "adjust", "thrive" and survive.

- Bobbi utilizes strengths developed in pre-retirement life to create a satisfying and meaningful new life stage.

THE ROUGH RIDER

"This should be my spring, but somehow I forgot to plant the right crops; nothing is growing that I recognize."
- Libby

Libby has always been one of the most fun-loving, joyful people one could ever meet - particularly for someone in the Human Resource (HR) field. Not that HR people are generally a dour or joyless lot, but HR can be a very tough job, particularly when the economy is bad and your department is responsible for laying people off, to say nothing of the general role HR plays in confrontation and performance issues. For most of her considerable time in the field she has maintained a great sense of playfulness and fun. Of the 30-plus years Libby has identified herself as an HR manager, 26 were spent in the for-profit arena and five were in the not-for-profit arena.

Libby would characterize the majority of her career as being one of helping people reach their full potential and removing unfair obstacles that would get in the way of their success. This was a very challenging, gratifying and fulfilling time for her. However, the last five years prior to retirement were certainly a rough ride. Her last two positions were in environments unlike any she had worked in before, not quite as sophisticated with regard to HR practices and she thought she could help them improve organizational performance by improving these practices. It didn't work out quite the way she intended: she ended up being let go from both these jobs. But there were valuable lessons to be learned even in these negative situations, and now she has some time to think about what she wants to do with the second half of her life.

Prior to retirement some of Libby's big concerns were: "…will I have enough money, will I still have the same friends and do the same activities?" Since retirement she has found, "there is never enough money, there is no time for me and everyone wants a piece of me since I'm 'retired' with 'nothing' to do."

When asked which of her thoughts since retirement had surprised her the most, she stated that not much surprised her since she knew herself pretty well. She realized she now had some time to think about what she wanted to do with the second half of her life, but she also admits, "I read the obits more. I need to stop doing that."

Libby urges women to "have a plan for your time as well as your money. I did not plan to retire now -- circumstances did it for me and now I find I am fearful of rejection, so I am not out there looking for work." She feels she identified herself too closely with what she "did for a living." Now Libby has to figure out who she is since she isn't working. As is true for so many Baby Boomer women, "I suppose because we were the ones who fought for changes, we confronted convention; we burned our bras. We then went out into the world and got a job as well as tending to all the other activities in our lives. When I look back I realize I *was* my job, so when I lost it -- *oh yes!* -- my self-esteem and identity were affected. I don't feel as powerful now; I'm really struggling with that loss."

Was there a new sense of freedom for Libby with this next phase of life? "I have not had freedom yet. I am still taking care of family members. But I think I have almost all of their problems solved now and I can begin to focus on me."

When it comes to family support Libby believes it can be a key to the success of one's retirement efforts. "My family wants me to be happy and do what I want to do however, they also want me to be at their beck and call." In her present situation, as she sees it, her family is a challenge to her enjoyment of this newfound "freedom." When she compared her retirement experience with that of her mother's Libby observed: "My mother had always worked. I don't think she really retired, she just quit looking for more work. Most of her friends, and family her age, passed away so it seems she just quit doing anything."

Long before she was anywhere near retirement age, Libby conjured the image of: "... 'La Dolce Vita' - the time in my life when I wouldn't have to work. I would travel to new and exciting places. I would ... *you know*... I don't know what I thought!" She's convinced now that retirement isn't what it was cracked up to be. Admittedly she wasn't prepared for it and had planned to work for at least another five years. "I had a goodly amount of money in my 401(k) and several pensions to rely on for money, but the economy tanked and took most of my funds with it." Because a job hunt may be on the horizon, Libby finds that rather than thinking of "retirement" as the correct term for this stage in her life -- terms like restart, rethink, regenerate, revitalize or renew seem more appropriate. Indeed, Libby has had a Rough Ride into the golden years.

SURVIVAL QUESTIONS:

1. How do you think you would have handled Libby's situation?

2. Did the description of Libby as fun-loving and joyful resonate in her story? Did the process of unplanned retirement alter her usually upbeat nature? Do you think she will regain her emotional equilibrium?

3. What stood out most in Libby's story for you?

OUR OBSERVATIONS:

- "Don't let people take advantage of your 'freedom'," is very wise advice even though this subject seems to be approaching the issue from a negative place.

- "Fear of rejection" when faced with the prospect of finding supplemental work is a disconnect from a history of major career accomplishments. Even much younger employers are often enlightened enough to value experience and skills in older candidates.

- Recognize that in this economy many more women may not have a choice of full retirement and accept the fact.

- As our Rough Rider suggests, "plant the right crops," so there is a lot to harvest when winter comes.

NOTE: For those readers who sensed that Libby wasn't really ready for retirement, she did overcome her insecurities about interviewing and is back at work in a for-profit business, leading an HR department again and happily creating a productive, fulfilling environment organization-wide.

PART TWO

BY THE BOOK:
OLD SCHOOL. OLD RULES

Despite the glut of "talking heads" prognosticating endlessly about the economy on news programs, blogs and eminent journals and publications, a Perfect Storm seemed to have overcome the financial world in 2010 quashing many a Boomer's dream of a leisurely retirement. But, with all the computer-modeling, instant information and rapid-fire response mechanisms at our fingertips, sometimes the "old way" of financial planning - plodding, cautious, deliberate, measured – proves to be at least as successful. Like a race between the turtle and the hare, the women whose stories you will read in Part Two, did their retirement planning for the most part, "by the book." Perhaps you can relate to their style or maybe you can learn from it.

The Disciplined Daughter

There's an iconic portrait of a woman and three young girls that was taken in the late 1950s for the cover of a local North Carolina newspaper. The photo shows the mother in a ruffled apron, her daughters gathered 'round as if to take in every word of wisdom she imparts while preparing holiday goodies. The woman and the young girls are impeccably coiffed, their clothes casual but crisply pressed. A typical suburban American kitchen scene -- mother and daughters happily baking, while dad is hard at work at the office. It's a photo that Martha treasures, as do her two sisters, because they were the models for the photograph.

Her mother would later divorce Martha's father at a time when divorce was still quite frowned upon, especially in the South, where they happened to be raising their family. But Martha's mother had no regrets and remained fiercely independent until her death in her mid-80s. The article that the photo illustrated represented an idealized version of their home life. Even then, the media could "spin" a story.

Martha is – as her mother before her – extremely disciplined. She explained that her mother's generation came out of World War II with low expectations: they worked hard and were rewarded with moderate pensions. They were conservative and didn't require as many things as her generation seems to need for happiness. "As an older 'boomer' we consumed and consumed! It will be even worse for my children and their children, as it is now much more difficult to attain the 'American Dream.' So I am happy I learned from a conservative mother."

But there were high times in North Carolina, to be sure! Martha, as a top executive in a major furniture company, had close professional associations with business representatives from across the US and many foreign countries, seeing to their showroom needs in the wholesale international home furnishing market, and then marketing the showroom and her company. This was a high profile position and she was highly regarded in the industry.

But after 28 years she had burned out.

Martha planned for her retirement early on in her career, always with an eye to leaving the business world by the time she was 62. And she was glad she had been able to apply the discipline her mother had modeled for her. In time she paid off her home and spent carefully so that when she retired she would be debt-free. She was an early proponent of the 401K savings program, believing that these measures would give her more flexibility when she retired. "Since I felt so burned out -- and as it turned out, the economy had 'gone south,' I was proud of the fact I could still retire at 62 and gain the freedom I needed."

Financial preparedness was the key to that freedom she wanted and felt she deserved after a total of 38 years in the work force. But now, current economic conditions (particularly the stock market) leave her feeling less confident than she had been initially. "I know I was prepared, but I also know that I might have to lower my style of living if the economy doesn't improve. Then there is the stress of where the retirement funds are invested, etc. So, in a way, even though I was prepared, money always plays a big role in everything. I tend to worry more about those matters now since my earning years are over and I need to grow what I have. There are no guarantees."

Martha reflects on this in relation to her own children as well, believing that they are becoming increasingly dependent on the government versus taking care of themselves, as she and her mother before her had: "I think they are in for a big surprise when the government can no longer support their lifestyles in old age. I believe the country has lost sight of the long-term benefits of hard work. They won't know the security of long years with one company. Maybe that's good – or bad – but I hope they begin to learn that only they can take care of themselves – not the government and not the parents." A cautionary note from a disciplined mom…

When she retired, Martha knew she would miss the interaction with work friends and business associates, but also looked forward to determining her own agenda. The sense of freedom that comes from retirement was a big factor for Martha, and in the years since she left her corporate position, she has really enjoyed setting her own agenda. "However," she admits, "I still find myself being the disciplined person I was throughout those 28 years of working for one company. It's difficult to change old habits. Now I struggle to allow myself the freedom I've earned. I still feel like I should be on the clock." There's that discipline gene again!

She also misses the "job well done" validation she was used to: "I no longer have positive reinforcement from the workplace." Yet she found it surprising how little she regretted leaving and how easy it was to move on to other things.

Well, not exactly. For the first two years of her retirement, Martha worked part-time helping to train her replacement – who had his own ideas of how to run things in her department. "I had expected it, so I wanted to let him do that. I learned early on that there is a time for all things, and I was ready." The extra income just when the market had tanked was welcome, even if the situation was somewhat uncomfortable.

Martha summed up her advice for women approaching their retirement years with words of wisdom that might just as easily have come from her own mother's Depression-era observations on life: "Prepare financially so you don't have that stress. Be certain to have an idea of activities and interests that will keep you busy. Don't look back – only forward. Take care of your health as much as you can so you can remain active and participate. Let go of the past relating to your career and work years and welcome the future!"

SURVIVAL QUESTIONS:

1. What do you relate to most with regard to Martha's story?
2. What stood out to you?
3. What did you find most valuable?

OUR OBSERVATIONS:

- Like Martha, it is not unnatural to be burned out after so many years!
- Martha had planned for the financial aspect of retirement but is very concerned due to lack of assurance about the market and investments
- Prepare financially to avoid stress.
- Identify activities and interests that will keep you busy.
- Don't look back – only forward.
- Take care of your health as much as you can to be able to remain active and participate.
- Let go of the past relating to your career and work years. Welcome the future!
- Martha likes the freedom to create her own agenda but still feels a sense of needing to be "on the clock."
- She misses the sense of feeling of a job well done and the positive feedback work offered.

THE CONSUMMATE PLANNER

If ever there were a woman with a plan, it would be Paula! Nothing in her purview escapes having a plan attached to it – from a hike, to an afternoon downtown for lunch and shopping. Even in retirement she maintains a detailed to-do list – although she admits that now, her to-dos are more often "should do, but don't have to do today." Ironically, being the queen of organization that she had become, Paula now can devote even more time to planning than before!

Given that she raised two children while working full-time and had to juggle all the competing responsibilities and perform that delicate balancing act that working women confront, it is understandable that she would develop superior organizational skills. While employed by a leading university in one of the country's largest university systems, her work involved the utmost discretion as well as "pretty relentless" problem solving.

How does someone with a 30-plus year career in academia make the transition from the need to plan every waking minute, to not needing a daily timetable to keep her life from spiraling out of control?

Like a long-distance runner who keeps jogging around a track even after crossing the finish line, Paula could not simply stop short the day after her retirement party. Her challenge is learning how to transition from someone who had no time to decompress and was always busy, to someone who has time for herself, is less scheduled and not rushing from one task to another.

Programmed for success from an early age – high school valedictorian to PhD. (Counseling Psychology) – Paula never slowed down her entire adult life until retiring. Even during the first few months after leaving the university she spent four to five hours a day clearing out a campus e-mail account so she didn't feel quite retired, although she appreciated not having to dash out the door every morning. After the e-mail project was complete she felt relief from the constant activity, high expectations, forced interactions with so many people (she supervised 26 people at one point in her career), unsolvable problems, the need to try to comfort or diffuse other's high levels of anxiety and distress.

"I have enjoyed slowing down my pace and being able to unload all of the current and historical University-related cases that circulated in my head. I feel much less guilty about spending time with my family and friends and doing things I enjoy. If the weather is great, I am free to get out in it and do whatever I want to do. The freedom to spend my days doing what I want to do is something that I have never experienced before, and I savor it each and every day."

Paula at first thought that retirement would provide time to clean closets and organize things at home (you can't keep a good organizer down!), but she finds she hasn't been doing much of that even though she has time for it now. All the non-professional activities she used to squeeze into her schedule such as musical theatre and opera productions, hiking and swimming, she now enjoys at a far more relaxed pace. She spends more time with the several adult children she and her significant other have between them. She continues to interact with colleagues from the university and participates in events there, which perhaps allows her to still feel connected to her "old" life.

Before her retirement, Paula had little time for herself. The incredible need for constant time management made her feel "boxed in," although she admits that she misses about 5% of her old identity and the challenges of her career. Being called on to give "expert" testimony in sensitive lawsuits and advising the upper echelons of the University regarding complaint facts and severity can be heady stuff. Also, she felt the extra work that some of these sensitive cases required allowed her to use her considerable skills in mediation and counseling.

Because Paula had from early youth, been a consummate planner, the fact that retirement seemed to be creeping up on her and she hadn't had time to plan for it, was cause for concern but she had not turned her attention in that direction. "I knew that retirement wasn't financially feasible until I was at least 58, also my jobs were extremely interesting, challenging and engaging, and for a long time I thrived on being a creative and competent professional in a stimulating university environment."

As the volume of cases and their nature began to change, Paula felt her job becoming more toxic, and she thought more and more about not being on campus full time. "I would have preferred to phase out more gradually into retirement, but that was not possible given the particular nature of my job and the university's budget crisis." Rather than weather the budgetary storm, she made the decision to retire, but she didn't have a fully-realized plan for doing so. However, being the planner that she is, she had long ago set up her finances within the University system to be sufficient for her needs when the time came to retire. "I intentionally stayed in my job long enough to create a situation where I knew that I could be relatively comfortable financially. I also refinanced my house just before I retired. I was able to free up some cash to make up for much of the monthly income I would lose by retiring."

Having now enjoyed the experience of retirement, the need to recapture some of her old "identity" has emerged. "Very recently, I have started to feel a bit restless and am having slight urges to re-engage professionally – not full time, but in some way that uses the skills that I spent so many years putting to use. I am spending more time thinking about how I could do something purposeful besides living my life." She admits to "rare moments" when she realizes that she doesn't have that identity any longer, and although it hasn't become a major issue, it's something she is very aware of. "I am not in a rush about this and I don't want to become overcommitted the way I was for so many years. But I'd like to do some work, whether paid or volunteer, outside the home that will keep me learning and growing and contributing to others in a meaningful way."

"My advice to women would be to spend some time prior to retirement thinking about what they are losing by retiring and what they might need to do to fill any voids that have been created by not working and use some of that pre-retirement time getting involved with organizations or activities." Sounds like a plan!

SURVIVAL QUESTIONS:

1. What discoveries did Paula make that you can relate to?

2. What thoughts have you given to the kinds of recommendations Paula makes about preparing for retirement?

3. What about Paula's story stood out to you the most?

OUR OBSERVATIONS:

- Explore in pre-retirement, some of the areas in which you think you might want to spend time.

- Examine the sense that, after being retired for a year or so, Paula needed to recapture some of her old identity.

- Paula has a sense of restlessness and need to grow and learn.

- The fact that her job was becoming more toxic helped Paula make the move.

- The incredible need for constant time management made her feel "boxed in," but still she misses a little of her old identity and the challenges of her career.

- The old titles and duties can be heady stuff. It may be hard to let that go.

- Paula now relishes the freedom: "to spend my days doing what I want to do. It's something that I have never experienced before now, and I savor it each and every day."

- Consider doing things that allow you to continue to feel a connection with your former life if that seems to be a need.

- How do you make that transition from so many demands to so few?

- Planning is a transferrable skill important in retirement.

⌘ ⌘ ⌘

Maybe there's something about people who are musical. The Left Brain dominance that's needed for the mathematical aspects of music, the precision, focus – all may contribute to a methodical approach to life in general, and retirement in particular? Well, it's only a theory! The next two stories are both about women who worked professionally in the field of music, who have both achieved extremely successful transitions from performance to retirement. See what you think.

THE PRAGMATIC PERFORMER

"You always know that at some point your 'instrument' will no longer serve you," observed Joan, a former opera singer. Similar to the on-stage longevity of a ballet dancer or pianist, for example, the human body eventually lets a performer know that regardless of how talented or well-trained, they have come to the end of their time in the spotlight. When this moment arrived for Joan, she was resolved emotionally to make the transition from performing to something else. "I had long before determined that I would not sing professionally when I couldn't trust my voice anymore."

Vivacious, with penetrating blue eyes and a passion for world-class music, Joan is an avid supporter of the local arts scene on the California coast where she and her husband reside in an elegant home, perched on a hill overlooking the Pacific Ocean. She has transformed her passion for singing to that of mentor, teacher, and philanthropist. "I come from a family of people who gave back to their community," she says. "My parents were not wealthy, but they gave of their time and talents, so I've always kept doing things wherever I've lived.

Joan grew up in Oregon, and began studying voice at 16. She earned a bachelor's degree in music and moved to San Francisco where she sang in churches and synagogues by day, and performed at the "Bocce Ball," an all-operatic nightclub in North Beach, at night. She saved enough money to travel to Europe and the Middle East for ten months where she received an offer to perform Mimi in "La Bohème" for the Istanbul Opera, opting instead to return home to get her Masters in Opera. "As an opera major, I learned that we 'did it all' – built sets, made costumes, and of course, sang!" Little did she realize that this would prove to be a good foundation for her later on in her career.

As the regional winner of the San Francisco Opera Auditions, she was accepted into the young artists' Merola Program, where she sang in "La Cenerentola." After a second year at USC, which included a summer performing the title role in "Madame Butterfly", Joan moved to Washington State to teach in a prestigious music conservatory. She married a musician and they moved to Nevada, where she sang with the newly-formed Nevada Opera Company. In 1968, they moved again and finally put down roots in California. Her career expanded to include concert performances along with opera productions, and then, when her husband took a sabbatical, she took a six-month hiatus to live in England. Constant travel is a given for anyone in the performing arts, and fortunately Joan had always loved traveling. She recently went on a three-week trip to South India by herself, armed with a new digital camera and lightweight laptop computer.

When she returned from England in 1987, she trained hard to get her voice back in shape and to sing onstage "one more time. It was the Mahler 2nd Symphony -- and it felt wonderful."

Because Joan had been involved in teaching and was a vocal coach throughout her career, she was able to continue working in her chosen art, giving master classes in Europe and China, adjudicating vocal competitions, and serving for 16 years as the director of a non-profit foundation that gave money to young musicians and local music organizations. It also brought world-class musicians to the area to perform for the public free of charge.

"I never wept a tear over the end of my vocal career. I always knew the time would come." By keeping in touch with everyone she met along the way, she built a large "opera family" who now provide support for one another as their own careers blossom and wane. The song may be over, but Joan is content: "The arts here are doing so well, and every time I look out at the view from my front window I think, ah, another day in paradise!"

SURVIVAL QUESTIONS:

1. What stood out to you with regard to Joan's life?
2. How do you think you would have handled the retirement from performing?
3. What did you relate to most in Joan's story?

OUR OBSERVATIONS:

- Joan is very realistic and therefore prepared well emotionally and literally for the transition to retirement. (Perhaps she has a High Emotional Intelligence Quotient, EQ).
- She successfully transferred her passion for her art to additional roles of mentor, teacher and philanthropist in the arena of her past career. (Known as transferring her Functional Skills)
- She built a strong networking group, which is now her support system.
- She recognizes her need for giving back and volunteering her time, talent and energy.
- She seems to have been very proactive her entire life.

And now, here's Lucy!

THE DO-RE-MI RETIREE

Lucy seems to have it all. Retired from her career as a choral conductor, she and her peripatetic husband now center their lives around travel, his business in the District of Columbia, and the activities of a dozen or so grandchildren scattered from coast to coast.

Her days are filled with music, meditation and one of her most treasured pastimes, reading. No longer conducting, Lucy sings with community choruses and church choirs wherever they land, which is currently in New York. For many years she conducted children's choirs in churches in the Midwest and East Coast.

Before she stepped off the podium, Lucy enjoyed work that gave her a great sense of fulfillment. But as someone who practices yoga and meditation daily, she is very content, and would describe her retirement as: "Ah…happiness at the luxury of not working!"

Lucy does admit to having missed having her own income – "until Social Security kicked in." Now she is able to enjoy her life even more, planning trips to exotic places like Viet Nam and frequent visits to all their children and adored "grandbabies." She and her husband are very comfortable visiting and staying in foreign countries – they once lived for a year in Mexico -- and Lucy often travels on her own, spending as much time as she can absorbing the culture of a place and learning as much as she can about its history, literature, and art. She is as likely to be as captivated reading a travel guide as she is the latest literary fiction.

Lucy is indeed one of the lucky ones who found great satisfaction and validation in her career and who now thoroughly appreciates her "time off." And she retired at the ripe young age of 53! Ohm...

SURVIVAL QUESTIONS:

1. What do you think/feel about Lucy's story?
2. What appealed to you most. Least?
3. Can you imagine yourself doing these things?

OUR OBSERVATIONS:

- Lucy was very satisfied and fulfilled in her work life and now feels the same way about her retirement life.
- She has time for leisure and fills her days with music, reading, meditation and travel.
- She has time for family.
- She sings with several choruses and reads about new places and cultures.
- Lucy is the perfect model for transitioning to retirement and enjoying it. It seems to be everything that she planned it would be.

Felicia's story is about planning ahead. She is approaching retirement and giving the entire process a lot of thought. Having worked in social services and women's issues throughout her career, she is particularly sensitive to women whose struggle is often for mere survival, much less quality of life.

THE RELUCTANT RETIREE

Felicia has Master's Degrees in both Social Work and Public Health. She is currently the Executive Director of an internationally respected women's association. She has enjoyed great success over the last 22 years, serving as Executive Director of two very different non-profit organizations. Not yet retired, but at 58, she is beginning to give it some thought. "I know this sounds so clichéd, but my dominant thought is, I'm not ready yet! Although the numbers of years say otherwise, I still feel so young in my career. The world is not yet sufficiently better, and that is what I devoted my life and career to. I'm not afraid of losing power – I don't define myself by those things – I just don't feel the fight is done."

Reflecting on what it is that has driven her career, Felicia commented: "I never thought making change happen would be so difficult. The first part of my life here, in this city, I worked in domestic violence prevention and intervention. We would make progress with leaders and then they would retire or die, and the system would revert right back to the way it was. Changing leadership – without having that leader work to change the rank and file – was never enough. I felt like I had done all I could and it was time for new leadership. I had made progress but the work of significantly reducing domestic and sexual violence was not complete. Now I'm trying to increase my community's awareness of racial justice issues as well as economic empowerment for women and it feels like starting all over again, increasing folk's comfort level to discuss this 'new' uncomfortable subject. Although change is urgent, it is not the same as running a crisis center. In this position I have time to think and hope I can start the wheels turning to create the skills needed for all people to become anti-racist allies."

Although she has yet to face the issue of retirement herself, Felicia had some sound advice for other women preparing for this change in career status: "Don't let your profession be you. Define yourself first in terms of what you personally bring to your profession. As individuals it's critical we see ourselves outside of what we do. That may be easier to understand intellectually than to actually achieve."

"I think family and friends are role models for how it (retirement) can be done well. My dad retired at age 70. His advice was don't retire before you are ready. My oldest brother (five years older than me) has announced his retirement in one year. That started the wheels turning for me – kind of a countdown question…will I be ready in 6 years? I have another brother 18- months older who is a psychiatrist and doesn't see his retirement in sight, and another brother seven years younger who was just made Dean at a prestigious college – so he isn't retiring anytime soon!" With regard to friends, she notes, "As a result of the stock market losses, many of my peers feel they will be working until age 70."

With few concerns about issues of identity, self-esteem or sense of freedom arising from a looming retirement, Felicia was mainly apprehensive about finances: she wondered would she and her husband have enough money and whether Medicare would be able to keep up with the growing number of baby boomers retiring in the next decade. She also has questions about where she might want to live. "I know I like the warmer climates of the South, but I want to surround myself with more liberal people than I have in the state I currently reside in." A potential move brings up a host of uneasy questions: "Do we want to move, and how difficult will it be to find friends and a support network."

Felicia doesn't feel she will miss her rather public role and even thinks she will welcome the anonymity that comes with being out of the public eye. She is looking forward to the time to explore short story writing and is looking forward to having the time to take classes or join a writing group. Additionally, since her husband traveled for most of his career, and travel doesn't provide much excitement for him, she is talking with a friend about places they would love to explore.

Retirement certainly has significant baggage that goes along with the outmoded perception of people over 55, but when approached about the physical aspects of the aging process, this highly-educated executive expressed an astonishing reservation: "Going totally gray will be a challenge. I exercise and feel good about my physical self and I'm not ready to be totally gray. For some reason I see that as a turning point of some kind. I think you become invisible when you are all gray and I'm not ready for that."

On a more pragmatic note, the role that money plays in Felicia's current life, and whether she thought it would change after retirement, is something she is able to face without hesitation. She has already become more frugal and thinks that in some ways the economic downturn might have been a blessing in disguise. Because of it, her family's spending habits have changed dramatically. She wants to save more now, in addition to her 401Ks, but doesn't want to turn into "one of those people who talks incessantly about their bargain shopping or savings." She doesn't want to lecture people or give advice when it isn't being asked of her.

As for female role models for successful retirement, Felicia lacks anyone close to her to turn to: "I lost my mother when I was 19 and she was 47 so I lost touch with her friends and didn't get to see up close and personal how they handled retirement. About half of her friends didn't have careers, just worked part time jobs. The other half worked in companies like AT&T and seem to have had comfortable, traditional retirement experiences. They traveled, volunteered and visited children.

"I see my generation as staying somehow connected more in the workplace through consulting, writing; I feel continued learning and growing will be an important part of my retirement life and experiences. I also think the internet and the ability to interact across the world will help us and future generations stay connected with co-workers nationally and internationally, allowing work to continue virtually if one so desires."

SURVIVAL QUESTIONS:

1. What stands out to you about this story?
2. What do you relate to most?
3. Do you think Felicia is a lot different than most Baby Boomer women, and if so, how?

OUR OBSERVATIONS:

- Felicia has some ironic - and seemingly contradictory feelings – fear of becoming invisible when "going grey" versus the "benefit of being out of the public eye."

- Dedication to a cause can be a life-long pursuit, and an inherent trait. Some people are focused on "the other" and not themselves.

- Many people worry that if they make a move to another part of the country for economic or health reasons later in life that they will have trouble making new friends.

NOTE: If anticipating a retirement move, here are some suggestions of pro-active measures to take in a new location: Take classes in subjects that interest you and you will find others with common interests. If you are a church-goer, you will quickly find a new church community; hobby groups like hiking clubs, book clubs, landscape artist groups again provide a known shared interest. Invite new neighbors over to get acquainted. Join a fitness club. Volunteer for organizations whose mission/activities interest you. Become a docent at an art museum. If there's a Newcomers Club join – if not, start one! Look for a part-time job. And remember, the impact of the internet on the ability to 'stay connected' can be a great reassurance and comfort to those displaced from their geographic comfort zones.

THE GOAL SETTER

From Fitness Instructor to Human Resources Manager at a Fortune 500 Corporation, this determined woman carved a very interesting career path for herself before her decision to retire a few years ago. After completing her Bachelors Degree in Human Potentiality, Marcia pursued a Masters Degree in Health Sciences. She then began her corporate career as a wellness program coordinator. Deciding next to become a Human Resources Representative, she made the change and over the course of the next 25 years Marcia was promoted to a variety of positions in the Human Resources Department. Contributing to the organization in many ways, she participated in organizational development initiatives, conducted training and development programs, and was involved in performance management, process improvement, staffing, employee relations and leadership development. She successfully managed all of the human resource functions and responsibilities for the organization.

To further her professional goals, Marcia obtained certifications as a Professional Human Resources (PHR) through the HR Certification

THE EMPTY DESK SURVIVAL GUIDE

Institute and Certified Performance Technologist (CPT) through the International Society for Performance Improvement.

Her outside interests have not changed from those she enjoyed prior to retirement, but now that she has retired, she has more time to really enjoy and pursue them. She spends time hiking, skiing, fly fishing, gardening, cooking, reading, traveling, doing photography, playing the guitar, taking fitness classes and playing with her golden retriever.

Prior to retirement Marcia says she was ready to leave the corporate environment and thought that she would eventually pursue a consulting position to stay challenged and involved. "The corporate world has a way of sucking the life out of you and stealing part of your soul if you aren't careful. I wanted time to re-define who I was and re-write a new script for myself."

Additionally, her parents and her older brother were very ill and she needed time to make certain they were cared for. She was also very concerned about the economy and the longevity of her nest egg since the financial crisis was looming just prior to her retirement.

Marcia learned the importance of goal setting twenty years ago when she and her husband utilized a goal setting tool she had learned and taught to employees. Using this tool, they analyzed and defined their top five values by which to live and work. These values also served as the basis for their retirement plan. The couple envisioned and wrote down their idea of retirement. They made financial choices and decisions throughout their careers to meet their retirement goals. "We developed our first retirement plan in our 30's. Through the years these values held pretty steady and were used as the litmus test for most of our financial and personal decisions. Financial security was one of our most important values. We hired a good money manager and consulted with several financial planners and tax advisors." Having a solid financial plan was critical for them. They also wrote out descriptions and examples of what they wanted their retirement life to be, look and feel like. Every year they read the plan to see if they were on target. "It was a work in progress and it evolved and changed as we did."

In spite of doing the professional goal setting, retirement held some surprises for her. One of the surprises was her notion of time. She hadn't realized how fast time goes and how elusive it can be. Immediately after she retired she said she needed to be unscheduled and uncommitted. She wanted some downtime to recover and recuperate. "I later found myself wondering what happened to all the things I wanted to get accomplished that didn't get done because I could always do them tomorrow". She also had visions of spending most of her time traveling, doing her hobbies and being in the great outdoors. However, Marcia got involved in care giving responsibilities as well as all of the house and personal business projects.

The original vision of a leisurely retirement life doing everything she dreamed of doing didn't quite turn out the way she thought it would. She learned that she wasn't as disciplined as she thought she would be when she wasn't meeting deadlines and soon realized the importance of planning and scheduling leisure time as you did when you were working. "It's too easy to put things off because we have more time than we've ever had and no sense of urgency."

Since retirement Marcia had another surprise for which she hadn't prepared. Most of her friends who work during the week were not available to spend time with her, so she rarely made it to the "slopes" the first year after retirement. She realized that she would have to find other avenues for social interactions and has since joined a hiking club and a fitness club where she has made new acquaintances with other retirees.

Another adjustment to retirement was getting used to not having a regular paycheck and withdrawing money out of her retirement plans. Even though she and her husband planned well for retirement and felt certain that they had a solid financial plan, she is still concerned about the economy and the security of their nest egg, given the current economy. Also, living with her spouse 24/7 has been an adjustment for both of them.

Her advice to others is to be clear on your goals and values and stay true to them. If you have a partner/spouse, make sure your goals and values are clear to each other and are in sync. Develop a retirement/financial plan early and start saving. Clearly define what you want from your life and what you want in retirement, and make a detailed plan for accomplishing it. Be flexible, consult with professionals and check your plan at least yearly.

Since her career played a key role in defining who she was, but not a major role, she reports no identity issues. She has stayed involved with her professional associations and committees to keep current with trends and issues in her fields of interest. She also keeps up her educational requirements for her certifications.

Her self-esteem has not diminished -- it has changed. She thinks of this as "reframing" how she defines herself. Her new definition involves being a good role model for her nieces and nephews since she has no children, and becoming a mentor to others. "I think of myself in a new and challenging role that is important in different ways than my role was as a career person."

She considers her new freedom as a "gift" of time to pursue what she wants to accomplish and experience. "My life is so much fuller and more enriched. I still have to compromise my freedom and time with my spouse and my family obligations, but that's easy compared to my career days."

Family support was an important consideration for Marcia and her spouse. Her parents and siblings were also supportive and played a big role in the retirement decision. In fact, her brother retired within the same time frame as she did. When asked about her mother's generation's view of retirement, Marcia said that most of the women she knew from her mother's generation were primarily stay-at-home moms. They had their own issues of identity and self worth, since their husbands were the primary breadwinners. Their job was in the home and they could "semi-retire" when the kids were raised and off on their own. She guesses that those women who had careers would have similar experiences to her generation of women.

She feels that the younger generation is "less devoted to selling their souls to their jobs and careers than my generation. They seem to have a healthier sense of priorities and work/life balance. They change careers and employers tenfold compared to our generation. They have technology on their side to help them work faster, smarter and be more flexible. They are more resourceful and not afraid of change." On the downside, Marcia notes, they also feel more entitled to getting the big jobs and the big bucks without 'paying their dues.' "My generation of women had to break through the glass ceiling to prove their worth in the work world. This generation of women is more accepted in those roles and don't have as big of a battle. The younger men are also taking a more active role in household duties and child rearing than our generation."

Retirement has given Marcia the opportunity to be introspective, redefine who she is, enjoy life more, smell the roses, and be involved in things that are important to her. "It's given me a new sense of freedom and renewal. Overall, my quality of life is enriched and more rewarding than it has ever been!" After a few years of being retired, Marcia offers these words as substitutes for "retirement": revitalization, rebirth, new beginnings, new awakenings or renewal. For her, this is also a wonderful gift of time to "search into your soul."

SURVIVAL QUESTIONS:

1. What stands out to you about this story?

2. What do you relate to most?

3. What did you think about Marcia's assessment of the Gen-X'ers? Do you agree, and if so, how does that make you feel about your own career path?

OUR OBSERVATIONS:

- Marcia took time to prepare for her retirement in her 30's. She envisioned what it would look and feel like, and she and her husband revisited her plan on a yearly basis over the years, making adjustments as their situation changed and their priorities changed too.

- Her outside interests in fitness and health haven't changed since retirement and tie back to her first career interest.

- After retirement she wanted time to redefine who she was and rewrite her script.

- Marcia learned how to goal-set early and used the same knowledge to assist in the retirement process which used values clarification.

- Marcia recognizes an issue of time management, in having more "free" time and less of a sense of urgency.

- Retirement surprises: Who can you spend time with when your old friends still work? Living with a spouse 24/7 is also a challenge.

- Be clear with goals and values and make sure those goals and values are clear to your partner and in sync.

- Marcia's self esteem hasn't diminished in retirement as she has reframed her role.

PART THREE

ENCORE! CAREER REDUX

In this section of the book, you will meet amazing women who took life skills and passions that were deep in their hearts, and transformed them into roles that will give meaning to their lives now and into the future. Their compassion, courage and concern about the world we live in is representative of those who can optimistically look outward rather than dwelling on the personal challenges that stem from growing older in a society that in general turns its back on those whose zenith of power and influence has passed.

THE DREAM CATCHER

Almost any weekend from May until November, you will find this remarkable woman and her equally remarkable husband at local Farmer's Markets and Community Fairs. Retired from her last "career" at age 50, she is now living her retirement dream - the dream to one day own her own business. A business that turned out to be a fairly unusual and uncommon one!

Linda spent her early career in several different occupations: Board Certified Hair Dresser, Board Certified Real Estate Agent and later, Retail Merchandiser. Always longing for something different, she dreamed of being independent and of starting her own business.

Linda disliked being inside all day and wanted to be active and outdoors most of the time. Early on she knew she enjoyed the country lifestyle, although she had never lived on a farm or was at all familiar with farm life. She also enjoyed gardening, crafts and sewing. The rest of the dream evolved over time: She was determined to find the right answer to fit her vision, researched her options, and found something she wanted to do that she knew she would enjoy. She also discovered what it would take to complete the task.

To prepare for her retirement, or rather her next career, Linda attended seminars and meetings on the rural lifestyle that she wished to pursue. She says that after much research, she determined what she wanted to do or accomplish in her "older years" and then proceeded to do just that.

The small business she and her husband developed and own, turned out to be a small farm in North Carolina! On their farm, they raise produce, goats, sheep, rabbits and other animals. They are beekeepers and soap makers and sell goat products such as specialty goat cheeses. They are regulars at the Farmer's Markets, selling their products and conversing with their customers regarding farming and their lifestyle. They are also involved in the *Agri-tourism* business and educating the public about modern farming methods, even hosting school children on tours of their operations. Very pleased with her choice, Linda says excitedly: "Farm life is wonderful! My schedule is determined by what needs to be done. Educating the public is both needed and enjoyable." The freedom to do what is both needed and enjoyable leaves her feeling that she has accomplished her dreams and goals: "My identity is my own as a small business owner -- farmer/beekeeper/soap maker. I am very pleased with it and how others perceive me to be. I maintain good self-esteem while educating the public and have the satisfaction of providing something of value. Others look to me and my spouse for beneficial information and useful products."

While her lifestyle is almost the same as when she retired, not having to work in a corporate world is a relief. Her time and schedule can be changed according to what comes up. "There is no need to rush around to get ready for work."

Family support was a critical component of Linda's preparations for her career transition. Without the support of a spouse or family member, she would not be where she is today. "It takes a lot of planning to prepare for another chapter in the book of life."

Her attitude about retirement differs from that of her mother's generation Linda observes: "I have more financial freedom than my mother did. Having no support from a spouse or family member made it harder for her to retire. I do not have to struggle to make ends meet and am under no pressure to keep up a lifestyle that I am not accustomed to having." She feels that the attitude of the younger generation is very different from both her mother's generation or the Baby Boomer women she knows. Labeling it "self indulgent," she perceives the next generation as not looking toward the future and vaguely having a notion that someone in the family would support them later in life. She does not see a lot of them sticking with a career or saving toward retirement, but rather living from day to day, with the hope that "something will fall into their lives" that will leave them independently wealthy.

When pressed, Linda substitutes the word "reorganization" for "retirement": "Although I am retired, I am more organized in my thoughts, feelings and priorities. Priorities have changed with aging. A 'job' or housekeeping is a lot less important than soap making or feeding livestock!" "Relaxed" would also be an appropriate description.

This "Dream Catcher" used a systematic process to identify what would make her happy and then created a life filled with meaning and purpose - a life that is full of fun and satisfaction. Her advice for others is to spend time doing research and discover something that you want to do and would enjoy and keep doing it. Then take time to plan carefully. Next, do it!

SURVIVAL QUESTIONS:

1. What did you find most interesting about this story?

2. Can you see yourself doing something like this, or another encore career? What sort of career would that be?

3. What do you think about the way she went about making her dream happen?

OUR OBSERVATIONS:

- Encore career? Oh, yes!

- She used a systematic process to identify what would make her happy and then created a life filled with meaning and purpose.

- She reframed her thinking to reflect "Reorganization" versus retirement.

- Linda recognizes the importance of a supportive family.

- Linda didn't think highly of the younger generation's attitudes. Do you?

- "It takes a lot of planning to prepare for another chapter in the book of life."

- While there are still external time demands on her, they are related to the needs of the clients and animals.

- She enjoys not having to rush or dress up, and that there are no corporate shackles!

THE EXPERIENCER

Donna has lived her entire life as an "experiencer." She has always felt that in order to learn about life she must first experience things for herself. From a very early age - growing up in Texas, she realized that she could not always trust another person's point of view: She'd learned that a person's experience of things is shaped by each individual's perspective and frame of reference. She was keenly aware that most often another's interpretation would be totally different than her own. (You will see how this attitude comes into play in Donna's life a little later on in her story.)

After receiving a B.A. and an M.A. in Theater, Donna completed post-graduate work in Education. Her adult life has been filled with a variety of careers, professions, positions, locations and situations. This plethora of experience has enriched her life and helped form a philosophy of life that is reflected in a pattern of seizing an opportunity as it presents itself and then "going with the flow." Try on this career cornucopia: Donna has been a college Speech, English, Theater and Journalism Instructor, started several children's theaters, worked with Arabian Horses and owned a ballroom dance studio! This remarkable woman has also been a writer, a newspaper columnist, a publisher, a farmer's wife, an entrepreneur and editor. Among the relationship roles that she has filled are daughter, wife, mother and caretaker. She lives with a deep spiritual conviction that she is in the right place at the right time which directs her to her spiritual purpose and mission at the time. Not surprisingly, she views the idea of "retirement" with the same conviction.

Although she says that she doesn't plan ahead, she was recently able to afford a move to Montana to care for her elderly parents, purchase an on-line magazine, and invest in a small business owned by her friends. Instead of "retiring," she will be spending the next stage of her life building the inspirational magazine and starting an on-line store, which will distribute World Wide Fair Trade Products. She feels that this is her current purpose.

Donna started a teaching career in Illinois, teaching speech and theater. After meeting a couple who raised and showed Arabian horses, she became involved in riding and showing them. She married (the first time) and moved to Texas where she taught theater at a Junior College and children's theater in a large and affluent city.

She divorced, moved to Kansas, started a children's theater program and subsequently got a high school teaching certification in order to teach drama. Donna then married a farmer, had a daughter and resigned from teaching. During this period, she worked with, and showed her Arabian mare. Upon returning to the world of work, she became a journalist and edited a four-page community supplement paper.

Are you keeping track of the variety of Donna's career pursuits? Wait, there's more: Donna divorced her second husband and moved to Wichita, where she substituted in area high schools and did some community theater acting. She became the director of a children's theater for a year. Then, after two very rough years with no steady employment she did some independent public relations work and speech consulting. Next she trained to be a ballroom dance teacher, moved to another state and opened a dance studio with her third husband. They operated the studio successfully for 12 years. Her husband became ill and they closed the studio and rented floor space so she could continue to teach dancing and care for him at home. During that time she also worked as an adjunct instructor. After a seven-year illness, her husband passed away.

Donna would describe herself as a spiritual person. Reluctant to offer advice because she is not sure that her attitude would work for everyone, Donna acknowledges: "I just firmly believe Jesus when he said, 'Seek first the kingdom of God and all these things will be added unto you.' My life experiences have simply born that out to be true". She believes that "If I work and focus my consciousness on doing the best I can with those opportunities I have, the physical needs will take care of themselves. In ten years, I should have a good income and since all my family is long-lived, I anticipate I will be around another 30 years at least."

For women who do concern themselves with future planning, she suggests they start the habit of saving money the moment they start working. For married women who identify mostly with their husbands, she says "start reframing your existence, focus on your individuality and become independent now!" Donna finds wisdom in the following aphorisms:

- DON'T BE AFRAID TO EXPERIENCE
- ALWAYS FOLLOW YOUR PASSION/INTERESTS
- TRUST TO THE UNIVERSE
- SEIZE OPPORTUNITIES

The best thing about this time of life for Donna is her sense of freedom finally to be herself. She says that her identity is just now becoming more centered and focused. Growing up as "the professor's daughter" Donna did not have the "foggiest notion" how to express who she was earlier in life. She is now able to realize and acknowledge that she is talented, beautiful, energetic and able to feel comfortable in her own power. She is functioning in totally new and different arenas and has met and related to people who are enthusiastic about knowing her now. Both her confidence and sense of self-esteem is increasing exponentially.

Donna feels that her father's life experience shaped her own attitude about retiring. He did not stop actively working until late in life and it is that model that has most influenced her. However, Donna's daughter and her son-in-law have a very different approach than she or her father. They are already planning and saving for their retirement. Although they are enjoying a nice lifestyle, they are committed to putting away a certain percentage of their combined income monthly.

For "The Experiencer" this is one of the best times of her life – a time that she likes to say is a "Post-65 Adventure."

SURVIVAL QUESTIONS:

1. What do you think was the best fit for Donna, in terms of a career?

2. Would you have taken so many career turns yourself?

3. How much does "go with the flow" impact your choices in life?

OUR OBSERVATIONS:

- The ability to perceive that other's perspectives may be different than hers seems to have informed Donna's decisions about career pursuits. A dance studio in Oklahoma? *Really!* Well, she and her husband made it work. Had she been highly influenced by other opinions her life might well not have been as adventuresome.

- She has had the drive/ability to seize opportunities, embracing (a wild) variety of pursuits and being open to taking on/

trying out new things. This bodes well for anyone in the position of having to examine their life situation and facing career change.

- Sometimes it takes a lifetime to make it all come together and "fit." Good news for retirement planning.

- She had a father who modeled the attitude to keep on working if that felt right and being open to the idea of doing new things. Her father is now 102 and her mother is 91.

THE VOLUNTEER EXTRAORDINAIRE

Curiosity about people, places, experiences and learning is what has guided our next "transitioner" through the choices that she's made during her interesting and diverse life. This curiosity and her passion for "Tikkum Olam," a Hebrew saying taught in her Jewish home as a child, have been driving forces throughout her life. "Tikkum Olam" teaches an obligation to repair and take care of the world whenever you see the need.

As was common with most Baby Boomer women, Patricia spent her first career in the educational arena, where she was an art teacher. She grew weary of the educational system, returning to graduate school to pursue an MA in Urban Planning and Policy. She spent fifteen years in the "for-profit" world as a Corporate Vice President in a health care insurance company where she managed a staff of 24.

But her heart really belonged to the non-profit world where the focus was on taking care of those in need and "doing important things for others." She had always spent her time and energy volunteering in the Jewish and non-religious sector, supporting a wide variety of children's activities, and serving as a board member on a variety of boards including a library, WITS (Working in the Schools Volunteers), and "Art Encounter." Using her passion for helping others, coupled with her strong social and networking skills, she also developed The Jewish Employment Network in conjunction with the Chicago Jewish Vocational Service, for Jewish Americans losing their jobs. In addition, she worked in a program that resettled Soviet Refugees in America.

Her boundless physical and mental energy allowed her to also start several "for-profit" businesses (all unfortunately non-profitable!) and utilizing her excellent administration skills, she set up and managed a medical practice for a solo practitioner.

Following the Katrina disaster, Patricia traveled to New Orleans with a group of colleagues and as you might expect, this trip gave rise to another non-profit organization. She now takes volunteer groups to New Orleans to assist in the recovery process and Jamaica to work with orphans. Initially, she networked with the congregants in her synagogue to help launch yet another organization. Their positive response and support assured Patricia that what she perceived as a need and a way to serve that need was right on target.

Patricia doesn't consider herself retired, just that she has left the for-profit world to continue her service to humanity in another manner. She now spends her time as President of her volunteer organization, which understandably, leaves little time for other pursuits. Still she is able to balance an enormous amount of non-profit activity with personal time for reading, playing bridge and canasta, helping her family (three adult children, seven grandchildren), and extensive travel (including 17 days hiking in the Himalayas). Pretty extraordinary, wouldn't you say!

As busy as she is, it would be hard to imagine that leaving the corporate world would have a negative impact on Patricia's self-esteem and her identity as a corporate executive. In fact, she has basically transferred her background experiences and skills into the non-profit sector and has been altered and reshaped by what she is doing at the time.

Keeping open to all life's possibilities is a value this active Boomer practices daily, taking the opportunity to continue to grow through adult education classes, learning new skills, and through the constant problem solving required in her day-to-day business. She also enjoys meeting new people as colleagues and clients, and spending time with her friends, entertaining, and daily exercise. Patricia is currently working on adding more trips for another non-profit volunteer travel group and is involved in an interfaith program which connects the congregations of a synagogue and a mosque.

Patricia has applied great wisdom to organizing this new phase of her life. She is meeting her need to find life's purpose through volunteering while remaining active in her physical, social, educational, leisure, and family arenas. Patricia offers this advice: "Continuously learn from others. Be fearless, don't be frightened, and reach out to others. Everyone must follow what is best for them, but keep the options open."

Patricia's mother never understood why she wanted to work at all, much less as hard as she does. Never having worked outside the home, her mother didn't have to concern herself with the issues of retirement. As she aged, she lost her driver's license and many physical skills and her options were limited. She slowed down considerably and for the last three years of her life she lived in a retirement community that she did not like. "It broke our hearts that she did not enjoy those last years. But a career was never a part of her life," Patricia notes sadly. Musing on the idea of her own retirement, Patricia says, "I had no idea that I would plan (or hope) to continue working with such passion and drive. I am very grateful." Although she has considered retirement several times, the idea of future retirement seems somewhat vague to her right now. "I find myself back in a working situation." She continues to welcome the challenges and discipline of a business that gives her great self-esteem and direction

-- as well as the support of her three adult children: "Their validation is very important. They think it's great. Many of my friends feel 'burnt-out' and welcome retirement and the freedom it offers. I may be there myself and may welcome it as a great time in my life, but it's not yet on my calendar."

Now single after a 43-year marriage, her profession keeps her busy, focused and growing. Her divorce settlement left her with adequate money to pursue the non-profit (with no salary). However, she remains careful and conservative with spending. She fears that retirement would provide too much freedom and unscheduled time, which may be a "downer" for her. As for freedom, "the way I have constructed it, my non-profit allows me as much free time and freedom as I require."

Another major consideration is health, which may dictate her future choices. "If I remain healthy and active my career experience may extend indefinitely." Looking forward, Patricia feels that the future may be exciting and very creative as we live in and create virtual work places: "It is thrilling to think of the options that will be available. Maybe everyone will be partially retired…all the time."

SURVIVAL QUESTIONS:

1. What values did you acquire early on in your life, like Patricia's drive to be of service to others?

2. Do you think that some people thrive on an "extreme" amount of activity? How do you feel about that?

3. Does Patricia's response to a perceived need resonate with you? Would you like to find some similar route of service to society that matched your life skills?

OUR OBSERVATIONS:

- Patricia's values gave her a unique focus on "the other" as an obligation, rather than an inherent desire.

- Volunteerism led her to a whole new life-long pursuit within the non-profit sector.

- She has gratitude for meaningful work — at any stage in life, really.

- Virtual work options have opened a huge new window of opportunity for those facing retirement. Patricia observed, "Maybe everyone will be partly retired...all the time."

THE CHANGE AGENT

"Finding space to rest and nourish myself was my primary goal for retirement. I had always worked in a 24/7 environment. I realized that I had physically and emotionally abused myself for several years and I needed to rekindle."

Trish retired for the *second* time at 59. Her first retirement wasn't exactly planned, but we'll talk more about this later. She had worked for a public utility for 23 years, with her first seven years in clerical positions, but ultimately rose to become one of the highest-ranking female executives in the company. She was one of what was commonly referred to in the 80's as a "superwoman" who raised her children, finished her degree, learned many new jobs, advanced up the corporate ladder, and maintained a spousal relationship that has lasted 45 years.

Trish, early in her career, had no idea of the depth and variety of the potential skills she possessed, to say nothing of the fact that not many career opportunities were available for women. This was a common story for many women of the Baby Boomer generation, but there was a movement afoot, even in the heartland, in the late 1980s, that would allow and even encourage, the selection and development of women who were willing to make the leap -- which meant facing the resistance and reaction that is part of change. She was willing to take the challenge and benefit from this transitional time.

After 20 years with the same organization, leading and developing thousands of people, garnering great promotions and ever-increasing responsibilities, her company was purchased by another holding company. She was asked to reapply for her current job by the buyer, and told she would have to move, if selected, to their corporate headquarters in another state or lose her job, which would have had a grave impact on her retirement plans. This phase of her career helped her gain a deeper understanding of both what her role had been in the old company, and would continue to be throughout her life: a "change agent."

It was this job transition that helped her realize on a very personal level, the need to appreciate and ensure that one's style fit a particular corporate culture. The jobs she had at her old company, and its culture, came with the requirement and expectation of innovation, information-sharing, and healthy confrontation. She had gotten used to, and enjoyed, the benefits of that type of environment. It only took 12 months for her to determine that a 'change agent' wasn't going to be successful in this new culture! For the first time in her career she was now getting performance feedback from a boss that was *not* positive and encouraging. The habits of sharing information with employees and building a participative team was not what was expected from leaders in this culture, and this behavior on Trish's part was viewed as inappropriate and had the contrary effect of making her new boss lose trust in her. Needless to say her career as a utility executive ended rather abruptly. Trish was offered an incredible severance package, was allowed to take early retirement and was able to negotiate the date for her retirement, staying on to help her successor prepare for his new position. "It still feels painful to discuss this time in my career," Trish admits.

At the same time this career shift was taking place Trish's mom died. She drove from Ohio to Kansas to attend to funeral arrangements and family. The time in her Mother's hometown with her sisters was spent crying and sharing personal items that belonged to her mother, mourning and grieving for both the loss of her dear mother and a big part of her identity.

On the return trip she was in an auto accident. She wasn't physically hurt, but the incident seems typical of the succession of incidents that often occur after major losses and changes in ones life.

Upon her return to the home she and her husband, a college professor, had maintained in a university town, she cried and grieved for about a month for all the losses she had suffered in the past year. Then she turned to creating the kind of home environment she envisioned for retirement. The changes started happening, first finding a more spacious place with a good yard for gardening. "Digging in the dirt at our new home offered me the therapy I needed at that time." She realized after she completed the new house projects that she wasn't ready to retire yet, but knew this small town market wasn't going to offer the opportunity or kind of money she had earned in the past.

Her next career move was to a hospital as Manager of Registration, Scheduling and Financial Assistance. What a challenge for the "Change Agent!" These were critical functions for the hospital, with a great deal of financial and customer service impact. "In three years, we moved the department from being considered the armpit of the hospital to being one of the most desirable places to work." Then a system installation brought her into some dysfunctional organizational dynamics, within another part of the hospital. She realized when she didn't have the desire and wasn't inclined to fight any more corporate fights, that it was the time to move into a new phase of her life that did include retiring. She had done what she set out to do in that environment and enjoyed the people and challenges. So Trish called her husband and told him she was resigning then and there, wrote a resignation letter, thanked her bosses for the opportunities, and left.

When this second career experience ended, Trish was ready to rekindle her personal interests. Initially it was wonderful reading a book all night and sleeping until noon, gardening, and just hanging out at home. " Eventually, I felt guilty due to my lack of participation in meaningful activity. I also felt aimless, I had *never* felt that way in my life." One of the major areas she struggled with was lack of day-to-day structure. But she knew it wasn't going to be the all or nothing approach that had been the situation earlier in her career, so now the burning question would be: "How do I reengage and still hold on to 'my' time?"

Trish has chosen to devote her volunteer time to work on projects she feels will make a difference for the people in the community where she now lives. One of those projects has included working with organizations on issues of aging and even lobbying the state legislature and setting up training for new legislators about the issues their aging constituents face. The "change agent" is at it again in a big way!

SURVIVAL QUESTIONS:

1. What strengths do you think Trish possessed at the time when the challenge was offered to her to enter into management positions that had not been available to women before?

2. Would you have accepted the offer to move to another state, to keep a job that paid even less than you were making?

3. Are you a change agent?

OUR OBSERVATIONS:

- Change agent is a perfect description for Trish!

- The objective to rest and nurture needs to be honored. At the same time when the need for meaningful activity arises, use that time to focus on skills you have that you want to put to use at this time versus finding/developing new skill sets.

- "Willingness to take the leap" is an essential characteristic for change.
- Allow time to feel/grieve/experience loss.

The last shall be first and the first shall be last: Our final profile is that of Jeannine, who was the very first person interviewed for this book, and whose comments and insight encouraged us to go forward with the project.

THE TRANSITIONER

During the warmer months in this iconic city in Utah, you can spot a physically fit, energetic Baby Boomer on the tennis court, biking, swimming or playing sports. She may also be seen hiking in the red canyons of Southern Utah. During the winter months, she will probably be seen cross-country skiing or downhill skiing on the slopes. Always engaged in exercise and physical fitness, Jeannine has not changed her pattern since she has retired.

As a single mother for most of her life, Jeannine's interest in physical fitness and exercise transferred to her daughter who became an Olympic Champion gymnast. In addition to her work, going back to school and raising an "Olympian" daughter, she also found time to knit, do handwork, read and volunteer.

After receiving her Masters Degree in Social Work, Jeannine worked as a Social Worker and Guidance Counselor in the school system for 27 years. During that time, she also worked as part of a special education team as an in-service trainer, teaching guidance curriculum.

According to Jeannine, after 27 years she was very ready to retire and try something new. She wanted to investigate something completely different and hoped to discover a new talent or interest, possibly pursuing the things that she wished she had studied and experienced when she was younger. One of her major concerns was that she would become out-of-touch with issues and become boring and stale. Staying active and involved became her most important priority: "I have never liked the phrase 'grow old gracefully'. I worked around hundreds of people of all ages and I feared a lack of stimulation and camaraderie when I retired. I had, and still have, a fear of not keeping up with technology and having new inventions sweep past me."

Since she retired, she is busier than ever, filling her time with volunteering at a local elementary school, serving as Board President of Friends of the Library and board member of Early Literacy Committee, and traveling on several humanitarian trips to Central America. She is also taking non-credit classes in anything that sounds fun and interesting and spending time with her two young granddaughters.

When asked about the role of money in her life, she replied that fortunately, the role of money has not changed. Now married, she feels she is one of the lucky people with the same income and good health insurance. "Health insurance is the biggest problem for people wanting to retire or change jobs. I know so many people who would love to change but cannot do so because of health insurance and, of course, right now the job market and the economy are not conducive to changing jobs or retiring."

Wanting to spend more constructive time at home and enjoy the quiet of her house, she is still searching for a balance of active and quiet: "It is harder to say 'no' to requests since everyone, and often myself, feel that since I am not working I have so much time on my hands. I don't often feel unproductive at home. I do find that I am much more relaxed and patient. I am not bothered at waiting times or slow drivers and I don't feel rushed all of the time. I think I live more in the present now, not always thinking and worrying about what I have to do and get done in a short amount of time. I really love sitting down and having a second cup of coffee in the morning instead of stopping at a fast take-out on the way to work. I read the paper more thoroughly and enjoy it more. Having more time is the key to everything. I feel that I do things better and more carefully. But I have not become a better cook or housekeeper, I must admit."

Jeannine misses several people at work and makes an effort to stay in touch with old friends. "When I run into people I used to work with they seem so happy to see me. But I have never missed the school system or the politics of the system!" After a few years, she really missed the children and started volunteering in kindergarten classes at a neighborhood school. "I thought that I would stay up late, watching old movies or reading, but I still turn in at a pretty early hour and get up at the same time I used to when I worked." (Soon-to-be retirees, take a mental note!)

Recognizing that indeed it *can* be lonely when everyone else is working or not available, Jeannine suggests keeping stacks of good books to read handy, or lists of small projects to do. Film Noir is one of her interests, and she makes sure to catch old movies that fit this genre. Also, she suggests getting involved in your neighborhood: "I met neighbors I didn't know before, just by being outside and walking around more."

Being fit herself, Jeannine advises not to wait until you retire to get in shape, get healthier, get stronger, lose weight or look for new interests or pursue things you've wanted to do: "Be 'ready to go' when you retire! Don't waste any precious retirement time. Health really is everything. If you aren't healthy you can't enjoy being retired and the opportunities that it brings. Take care of your health now."

Mastering the steps to a successful transition, Jeannine suggests starting to cut back work hours in order to ease into retirement. She also recommends a lot of pre-action-planning. One process she used was to map out various areas of her life and survey: "Things That I

Did," "Things I Wanted to Keep Doing" and "New Areas of Interest." She included these categories: Health/Physical; Intellectual, Self-expression, Recreation and Fun, Creative, and Civic Involvement.

From time to time, she consults these charts to see how she is doing and to make modifications. Before she retired she started a few new things, playing tennis again, and taking a few classes. She also talked about retiring with others who were in the same stage of life to get ideas from them. They talked about what types of things they wanted to do with their time. "Having a support system was very helpful to me and I suggest that people thinking about retiring really look at theirs."

Jeannine's attitude toward retirement is in direct contrast to that of her mother. Her mother had a very difficult time retiring and she did so only when she really had to. Since work as an office manager brought her recognition that she did not receive elsewhere, her whole sense of self was wrapped up in her work. After retirement she was "lost' for a while and constantly relived her working hours. Eventually she found a few other things to do but she basically sat around, went shopping, or watched TV.

Although Jeannine's experience of retirement and self-image issues are different than her mom's, she is developing a new sense of self.

"I have noticed now more than ever before that the first thing people ask when you meet them is 'What do you do?' It can put you on the defensive so quickly and make you feel that you have to justify yourself. It can be a very judgmental question. I really feel for women who work as homemakers and mothers! Then I was asked once, 'How do you spend your time?' It was a wonderful question! You can answer anything to that! I try to always use that now and never ask what someone does (implying work). I still find it difficult when I am in a group of people who are all working and talking about their work. It is difficult for me to be part of the conversation.

I avoid some situations where I know that will happen. However, many people are truly impressed with what I did and that is helpful. Self-esteem can become a real issue and it does get to me once in a while, if I feel that I am not being productive or contributing to society. I think that it is important to do meaningful volunteer work if you can."

Enthusiastic about her retirement life, she is experiencing a wonderful sense of freedom. She feels much more in control of herself and her situation and can pursue her life the way she wants. "I feel that I am still doing the things that I believe in and want to be involved in, but on my own terms. I enjoy my time with people more than before and am grateful for the time I have to spend with my grand-daughters and the time I had to spend with my mother before she died. It is so much easier to travel now and it is so much more fulfilling. The task is to stay healthy and strong to do all of the things available now." Wisdom from a friend we can all take to heart.

SURVIVAL QUESTIONS:

1. Which of Jeannine's practical tips about retirement were most helpful to you?

2. What factors have made her retirement work successful for her?

3. Do you think Jeannine's lifestyle is attainable for everyone? If not, why not? If not, what changes would be necessary to be able to achieve a similar retirement scenario?

OUR OBSERVATIONS:

- Jeannine is pragmatic and practical, and very self-aware. She knows her limitations, sees the potential for problems and deals with them in a very logical, down-to-earth way.

- She has great suggestions.

- Like several of our interviewees, she has an "attitude of gratitude."

- She makes an effort to keep in touch with former colleagues she likes, to get out and meet new people, and to use her career skills to good advantage as a volunteer.

PART FOUR

Your Personal Survival Tool Kit For Women Planning To Retire, Already Retired, Or Considering A Career Encore.

FACT: 78 million Baby Boomers will retire over the next 20 years!

As Baby Boomer Women, depending on when you choose to retire, you may have 30-plus years ahead of you in this next stage of your life. This is probably longer than any of your other previous life stages. Living longer gives you more opportunities, as Bruce Springsteen says, "… to make it real."

Most retirees plan for their financial needs and dream about leisure activities, but do not plan for other important areas of life in retirement. Using this EMPTY DESK SURVIVAL TOOLKIT, which is based on lessons from our Baby Boomer interviewees, additional research and our own experiences, will assist you in including all the life areas and prepare and plan for a satisfying and meaningful career encore or retirement life.

THE THREE MOST IMPORTANT QUESTIONS OF "RETIREMENT LIFE"

E arly career development gurus introduced the three most important questions a person should answer before making career decisions. However, these questions should also be answered in preparation for making any life transition or decision. Answering these questions has become one of the biggest value-added processes one can complete at various life stages. It is especially important now, at this juncture in your life, to complete this process before you start your retirement (or encore career) journey. Answering these questions will help you to:

LIVE YOUR RETIREMENT LIFE ON PURPOSE, NOT BY DEFAULT:

Taking the time to answer these questions will allow you not only to survive, but to live this unique period of your life "on purpose," not by "default." If you carefully think these questions through you will be able to live a retirement life based on clear intentions and with great satisfaction. You have an opportunity to redefine yourself and your purpose in retirement while embracing a new found freedom.

The questions seem very simple, but require a great deal of thought and consideration. Your answers will help you create the foundation to build a successful retirement life.

ADOPT A POSITIVE ATTITUDE:

Having a positive attitude sounds like a cliché, but is a very necessary element in any kind of successful planning. Think about entering this stage of your life as a positive adventure in which you now have the luxury of setting clear intentions, aligning your values with your decisions and creating a satisfying plan for the next phase of your life that should be revised as needed.

REDEFINE "SUCCESS" IN RETIREMENT OR AN "ENCORE" CAREER:

The meaning of the word "SUCCESS" is an arbitrary one which we continually redefine as we move through various life stages and situations. Our definition of "Success" as we related it to our working life is no longer valid in our retirement life. You now have an opportunity to "reframe" or take another look at how you will define a "successful" retirement life. After completing the exercises in this EMPTY DESK SURVIVAL TOOLKIT you will be able to develop a new concept of "success."

ACKNOWLEDGE YOUR NEW-FOUND POWER AND FREEDOM:

Many of the interviewees mentioned the dichotomy they are experiencing in retirement between a new-found freedom and sense of power this brings and also feeling a sense of loss of power or identity. The key here seems to be to focus on the sense of being free of the limitations imposed by others and job responsibilities. You can learn to appreciate and successfully manage this aspect of retirement, which rewards you with a sense of power to control your own destiny.

DO SOMETHING WONDERFUL:

"One thing I know: the only ones among you who will really be happy are those who have sought and found how to serve." --Dr. Albert Schweitzer

This could be a time for you to use this freedom and power to be innovative and accomplish something wonderful in the world. This time of your life is an opportunity to direct your energy outward and make a contribution and a difference. In his book, "The Seven Spiritual Laws of Yoga," Deepak Chopra suggests that we ask ourselves an additional question: "How can I serve?" Hundreds of opportunities to serve are listed on the internet and include: Peace Corps, Senior Corps, AmeriCorps, Global Volunteers, RSVP, AARP and many others.

QUESTION ONE: WHO AM I NOW?

WHILE YOUR PAST IS PART OF YOU, IT SHOULD NOT DEFINE YOU NOW!

You may think you know the answer to this question immediately, but this is a very complex question. Even if you think you know who you *were*, you must answer this question in "real time." As Baby Boomer Women, we have been constantly evolving, based on our professions, circumstances, life experiences, and current life stages. A helpful first step in answering this question is to complete the following Values Identification Exercise to discover your "authentic self" and WHO YOU ARE NOW!

SELF-ASSESSMENT/VALUES IDENTIFICATION

We are value-programmed with our core values at an early age, but despite what you might assume, some of your core values can and have changed as you have grown into the person you are today. Since there are many categories of values, i.e. personal, life, ethical, social, career, and work, it is important to check and be certain that you know what your current values are.

EMPTY DESK SURVIVAL WORKSHEET #1:

VALUES EXERCISE: WHAT ARE MY CURRENT VALUES?

Values can be defined as the "foundation on which your life is set." Your values usually determine your perceptions, beliefs, reactions or responses to people and experiences. Considering your values should be an important part of your career encore or retirement planning in order to ensure that your choices are aligned with your core values. The following exercise will assist you in identifying the values that are most important to you at this stage of your life.

Review the list of COMMON PERSONAL VALUES and put a check mark in the box for each of the top ten that are most significant to you.

COMMON PERSONAL VALUES

Adventure	Challenge	Change	Creativity	Family Happiness
Financial Security	Freedom	Friendships	Geographic Location	Health/Personal Safety
Independence	Integrity	Leisure	Leadership	Intellectual Activities
Money/Wealth	Physical Activity	Recognition	Religion	Personal Growth/ Development
Service	Spiritual Growth	Travel	Variety	Volunteering
Others/Not Listed:				

List the top ten in the Values Weighting Exercise chart and rate each value by placing a check in the appropriate column. (Additional resources for identifying your values can be found in our Resources Section and on the internet.)

VALUES WEIGHTING EXERCISE

VALUES	ALWAYS VALUED	OFTEN VALUED	SOMETIMES VALUED	RARELY VALUED
1.				
2.				
3.				
4.				
5.				
6.				
7.				
8.				
9.				
10.				

List your top five values:

_____

_____

_____

_____

_____

_____

_____

_____

_____

_____

QUESTION:
When YOU make a decision to do something, do
you ensure that the decision is aligned with YOUR
current values?

SELF-ASSESSMENT/ IDENTIFYING YOUR STRENGTHS AND SKILLS:

The next step in understanding "Who Am I Now?" is to identify and analyze your current strengths and skills. Researchers have identified our skills and categorized them into three types as follows:

1. Personality Skills - traits which you were born with or acquire at an early age (Social Skills, Mechanical Skills, Organization Skills),

2. Transferrable Skills - those you develop and can transfer from one place or situation to another (Basic Computer Skills, Leadership Skills, Conducting a Meeting, Project Management Skills)

3. Technical Skills - those related to the knowledge of a specific job (Mechanical Engineering, Information Technology, Public Relations).

Most likely, by this time in your life, you have had an opportunity to recognize and utilize your most obvious and dominant skills, which have become your strengths. These are the personality traits and other skills that you have used, learned and developed in your career and life.

The following exercise provides an opportunity for you to review these strengths, identify those that give you satisfaction and enjoyment, and those you have used but do not enjoy or desire to continue to use. It is also a time to discover other strengths you would like to use or develop but have not had the chance or taken the time to develop.

Now is the time to reassess those strengths (also referred to as Knowledge, Skills and Abilities) and decide which will determine the direction you will choose to take in retirement.

EMPTY DESK SURVIVAL WORKSHEET #2

WHAT ARE MY CURRENT STRENGTHS?

This exercise will get you started identifying your preferred strengths. Take a separate sheet of paper and write your responses to the following questions:

1. What are my current strengths? Include your personality traits, your transferrable skills and your technical skills.

2. What makes me think these are my current strengths?

3. What accomplishment(s) am I most proud of? What strengths (knowledge, skills and abilities) did I use?

4. What strengths have others recognized in me?

5. Which strengths do I enjoy using?

6. Which of the above do I want to keep doing?

7. Is there a knowledge, skill or ability I want to develop further?

QUESTION:
When you make a decision to do something, do you ensure the decision is aligned with the strengths and skills you prefer to use? There are many other resources that can give you a more in-depth look at your strengths. Refer to the Resources Section of this book.

EMPTY DESK SURVIVAL WORKSHEET #3

WHAT ARE MY CURRENT INTERESTS?

SELF-ASSESSMENT/IDENTIFYING CURRENT INTERESTS/PASSIONS

Now that you have reviewed your values and strengths, it makes sense to discover and identify your current interests and passions to ensure you also include them into your Retirement Survival Planning.

"PASSION" is defined as "a deep overwhelming feeling or emotion".

You have the best possibility of success when you follow the things you are passionate about. At this point in your life, you probably have developed a variety of satisfying interests and possibly have one about which you are passionate. There is now time to recommit to those interests or to search for and develop other new and exciting interests and passions.

Write your answers to the following questions on a separate sheet of paper to help you identify your interests and passions:

1. What are my current interests and passions?
2. What activities do I currently enjoy?
3. Is there an interest or passion from the past I want to renew?
4. Do I have a new interest or passion?
5. Which interests or ideas fill me with energy?
6. What has given my life meaning and purpose?
7. What will give my life meaning and purpose in the future?
8. List five things you love to do.

YOU WILL BE MOST SUCCESSFUL AND SATISFIED IF YOU "GO WHERE YOUR ENERGY IS!"

QUESTION:
When you make a decision to do something, do you ensure the decision is aligned with your current interests and passions?

The next part of the exercise will help you make sense of the assessment information you have completed so far.

EMPTY DESK SURVIVAL WORKSHEET #4

SELF- ASSESSMENT SUMMARY SHEET

VALUES:

Review your VALUES Worksheet and write down your top five values.

_____

_____

_____

_____

How will you ensure that you will be honoring your values and aligning them with your CAREER ENCORE/RETIREMENT PLANNING DECISIONS?

_____

_____

_____

_____

STRENGTHS:

Review your STRENGTH Worksheet and list those that you want to use in retirement:

_____

_____

_____

_____

How will you use your preferred strengths in your RETIREMENT?

_____

_____

_____

_____

INTERESTS/PASSIONS:

Review your INTERESTS/PASSIONS Worksheet and summarize them.

_____

_____

_____

_____

Which INTERESTS/PASSIONS will you pursue in Retirement? Why?

_____

_____

_____

_____

After reviewing the stories of the interviewees, who do you think did the best job of matching their VALUES, STRENGTHS, INTERESTS/ PASSIONS to their career encore or retirement decisions?

QUESTION TWO: WHAT DO I WANT?

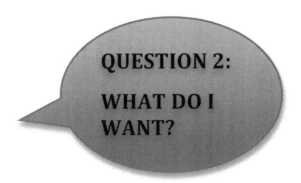

"Life is what happens while you are busy making plans."
- John Lennon

As you know, any strength can become a weakness if it is overused and planning is one of those strengths, as Lennon's quote implies. But at this juncture some assessment and planning are necessary and if you do not already know the answer to this question, "WHAT DO I WANT?" you must enter The Exploration Phase. The Exploration Phase requires introspection, visualization, life areas satisfaction assessment and research to clarify your retirement goals. You will be clarifying your answer in this next section.

EXPLORATION: INTROSPECTION EXERCISE

Review your answers on the "Self-Assessment Worksheet" you completed earlier, keeping in mind your identified values, strengths, interests and passions as you answer the questions below. Use a separate sheet of paper to record your answers.

1. What have you always enjoyed doing and want to keep on doing?
2. What have you always wanted to do, but have not yet done?

3. What have you been doing that you no longer want to do?

4. Is this the opportunity to give back and serve in some capacity? How will you do this?

"IF WE ALL DID WHAT WE ARE CAPABLE OF DOING, WE WOULD ASTOUND OURSELVES." Author Unknown

ADDITIONAL EXPLORATION EXERCISE:

Some of our interviewees used their retirement planning time to create and begin "encore" careers.

Following are some additional "WHAT DO I WANT?" questions to assist you in exploring this possibility:

1. Do I want to continue working? If yes, do I want to work full or part-time?

2. Do I want to continue working in the same job or a different job or field?

3. Do I want to transfer my preferred strengths/skills to a different job or field?

4. Do I want to get retraining or go back to school?

5. Do I want to work at home?

6. Do I want to explore my passion?

7. Do I want to create my own job or business or buy a franchise?

8. Do I want to turn my hobby or interest into a business?

9. Do I want to explore an entirely new interest? If so, what will that be?

EXPLORATION:
VISUALIZATION EXERCISE

The process of visualization can often assist you in clarifying what you really want. Read the description of the visualization exercise below and then close your eyes and visualize yourself in each situation. Better yet, have a partner walk you through it as you close your eyes.

INSTRUCTIONS:

- Imagine yourself five years from now in a place that makes you feel happy.

- When you wake up in the morning, look around and notice your surroundings, what are you wearing, who is with you?

- Get dressed for the day. How are you dressing? Where do you plan to go?

- Walk through your house. Notice details about the rooms you are entering. Who else is in the house?

- After breakfast, how do you begin your day? What are you doing today? If you are going someplace, where are you going?

- Walk yourself through the day. Who do you interact with? What do you do?

- Are you feeling satisfied?

- Return to the evening meal. Where are you? Who is with you? How do you feel about this day?

You can work through this exercise as many times as you need in order to discover the answers to "What Do I Want?"

What did your visualization reveal to you?

How can you use this information in your retirement planning?

EXPLORATION:
"WHEEL OF RETIREMENT LIFE"

Each area of our lives, identified and categorized differently by numerous researchers and coaches, comprise an entire "wheel of life." The following wheel is our version of what we call the "Wheel of Retirement Life." In order to make good retirement decisions, you need to review and then assess your current satisfaction level in each of these areas.

Once you have reviewed the explanations of the areas listed, complete the "Wheel of Retirement Life" exercise.

Wheel of "Retirement" Life

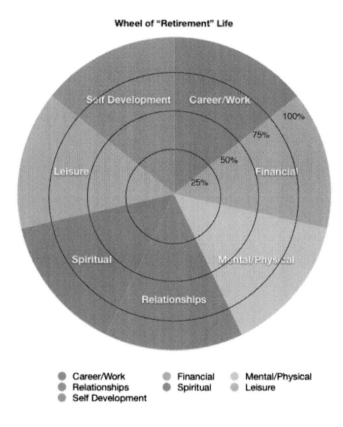

● Career/Work   ● Financial   ● Mental/Physical
● Relationships ● Spiritual ● Leisure
● Self Development

LIFE AREAS

1. Career/Work Replacement:

Researchers identify five losses a person can experience when leaving a job, whether it is voluntary, involuntary or as a retiree. There are numerous ways in which you can replace these losses, depending on the intentional decisions you make, as is evidenced by our interviewees. These losses are generally accepted as:

1. Compensation

2. Meaning (Contribution or Sense of Purpose)

3. Structure (Time Management)

4. Status (Self-Worth)

5. Socialization (Social Needs)

2. Financial:

Of course, you must be able to support yourself financially in order to be able to retire. Your retirement savings may have suffered due to the recent economic recession and you may have to work longer in order to rebuild your retirement assets. It is recommended that you seek advice from a Financial Planner in order to assess your financial situation. You will need to confer with your accountant, insurance representative, banker and anyone else who handles your money to be certain that you understand your tax liabilities. You will need to answer questions such as: How much money do I need? How will I ensure that my financial needs are met? What insurance coverage will I need? When should I apply for Social Security? What is the best thing to do with my 401 Ks, IRAs, Annuities, etc.?

3. Mental and Physical Health:

The importance of staying healthy, mentally and physically was mentioned by most of the women. You must take care of your mental and physical well-being if you are going to enjoy a successful retirement life. A nutritious diet and physical exercise are part of a healthy retirement life style. An additional health related issue you might have to consider, which surprised several of our interviewees, was the need to become a caretaker for a family member.

4. Relationships:

Maintaining and building healthy relationships are important throughout life and should continue in retirement. Several of the interviewees depended on their extensive social networks and also started developing new networks. One suggestion was to develop a support group to assist in making the transition. In this social networking world there are many Baby Boomer websites and blogs already operating and new ones are being created each day. Additional opportunities to meet new people and make new friends can increase through time spent in old and new interests. The need for supportive family and social relationships was emphasized. This is a time when relationships with family members and friends have time to develop and heal.

To avoid some of the boundary issues experienced by our interviewees, you must get clear about your desires and needs and set boundaries with family members and friends when necessary.

5. Spiritual:

Your spiritual self is very personal and often private. You have your own definition of "spiritual" and need to explore its meaning for yourself. Once you complete the wheel and have a graphic picture of how you are choosing to spend your life, you will begin to notice that the areas of life overlap one another. As you discover what gives you meaning and purpose in retirement, you will notice that this will affect the other areas. Perhaps you will commit to aiding some cause about which you are passionate, or devote your time to improving the life of another. If you have the intention, you will find a way to serve!

6. Leisure:

Many of you have dreams of how you plan to use your leisure time in retirement. As you can see, from our stories, many do not have as much leisure time as they planned to have. Leisure has to be programmed into your schedule or it will disappear. Many use this time for traveling, ecotourism, hobbies, education, volunteering, providing community service, reading, sports or pursuing a new or rekindled interest or passion. With new- found freedom is this your time to do something wonderful?

7. Self-Development:

Self-Development can include spiritual or charitable endeavors or pursuing more concrete interests. Many of our Baby Boomers have adopted a philosophy of life-long learning, which enriches their retirement lives. Retirement is the perfect time to explore and discover your passions or purpose, participate in a variety of intellectual activities or pursue another degree. Most colleges and universities offer lifelong learning programs or other exciting classes and programs for seniors. There are numerous educational, volunteer and travel experiences listed on the internet.

EXPLORATION:
"WHEEL OF RETIREMENT LIFE"
EXERCISE

C omplete the "Wheel of Retirement Life" on page 106 to assess your current satisfaction level in each Life Area. Use the concentric circles, as a guide and color in the correct percentage of satisfaction that you are feeling in each area from 0% to 100%. You will then have a graphic picture to review for this exercise. Those of you not yet retired can complete the exercise for a current and a future view.

After you complete the "Wheel of Retirement Life" exercise, answer the questions below to help you identify those areas in which you want to change your level of satisfaction.

1. Identify the areas of satisfaction.

2. Identify the areas in which you are not satisfied.

3. Identify and list areas you want to change.

4. What can you do to raise your level of satisfaction in each area?

EXPLORATION: RESEARCH

The last step in exploration is to research your discoveries. Once you review your self-assessment results and complete the exploration exercises, you will have a direction for your research. There are a plethora of resources available. The libraries and internet are filled with information and resources. Books, websites and blogs are easily found, some are referenced in the Resources Section. Classes and Workshops are offered at most colleges and universities. Retirement coaches are available to assist you further. So you are ready to set your GPS to reach your destination.

QUESTION:
Which of the interviewees spent time exploring and researching their retirement options?

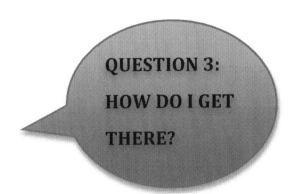

LETTING GO OF THE PAST TO MAKE WAY FOR THE FUTURE:

The first thing you may have to do before answering this third question is to make room for the next chapter in your life. You will need to let go of some of the past images you have had of yourself in order to envision the new one that better matches what you want to create. There may be a part of your professional self-image that will no longer work for you or is no longer providing you satisfaction and a sense of fulfillment. If you adhere too closely to who you thought you were, or who you actually were before retirement, you may lose out on an entirely new opportunity to create something new and more rewarding to you now. Letting go of the past also means an opportunity to redefine "success" in the future.

Next, be certain your retirement decisions are in alignment with your answers to the first two questions, "WHO AM I NOW?" and "WHAT DO I WANT?" Honoring your new or renewed values, strengths, interests and passions and your vision of what you want in your retirement life will ensure that you will do more than survive retirement. You will live your retirement life intentionally and "on purpose."

You can begin answering the question "HOW DO I GET THERE? after thoughtful and purposeful introspection, exploration, research and planning. Refer to the Resources Section for further information to get you started

Finally, completing the following RETIREMENT SURVIVAL ACTION PLAN will help you summarize the work you did in the preceding exercises and develop an Action Plan to use to make your ideal retirement life a reality.

My Retirement
Survival Action Plan

"**Y**our Vision will become clear only when you look into your heart. Who looks outside, dreams, who looks inside awakens." - Carl Jung

Based on the previous discussions and exercises respond to the following questions on a blank sheet of paper:

1. HOW WILL YOU REDEFINE "SUCCESS" IN RETIREMENT? (THIS STATEMENT ALSO BECOMES YOUR RETIREMENT VISION STATEMENT)

2. HOW WILL YOU REPLACE EACH OF THESE WORKPLACE LOSSES?
   a. COMPENSATION
   b. MEANING/PURPOSE
   c. STRUCTURE
   d. STATUS
   e. SOCIALIZATION

3. ANSWER THE THREE QUESTIONS OF RETIREMENT LIFE:
   - WHO AM I NOW? (ANSWER BASED ON YOUR SELF-ASSESSMENT SUMMARY.)
   - WHAT DO I WANT IN RETIREMENT? (ANSWERS BASED ON THE EXPLORATION SHEET EXERCISES.)
   - HOW DO I GET THERE?

Transfer the Retirement Life Wheel Areas to a page arranged similarly to the following topics, leaving space for 1 to 3 goals in each area along with space for the action plan to advance the goal. Then set goals for each.

You may customize the labels by changing, adding or subtracting areas to match your own life wheel.

Establish 1 to 3 goals in each area depending on how satisfied you are with that area in your life. Then add the action steps to support those goals for example:

WHEEL AREA 1: CAREER/WORK REPLACEMENT

Goals: 1. Have a plan to replace the five job losses.

Example:

a. Compensation: Make an appointment with my financial advisor to plan for a monthly withdrawal of funds (Date).

b. Meaning and Purpose: Investigate at least two newly-identified interests that will give me meaning and purpose by (Date)

c. Structure: Plan a daily and weekly schedule that includes exercise and a healthy diet (every Monday)

d. Status: Accept the offer to join the hospital board of directors. Call Alice by (Date)

e. Socialization: Plan a monthly lunch date with alums (Date)

WHEEL AREA 2: FINANCIAL

GOALS:

ACTIONS:

WHEEL AREA 3: MENTAL/PHYSICAL HEALTH

GOALS:

ACTIONS:

WHEEL AREA 4: RELATIONSHIPS

GOALS:

ACTIONS:

WHEEL AREA 5: SPIRITUAL

GOALS:

ACTIONS:

WHEEL AREA 6: LEISURE

GOALS:

ACTIONS:

WHEEL AREA 7: SELF-DEVELOPMENT

GOALS:

ACTIONS:

DECLARE YOUR INTENTION

Now that you have answered the three most important questions of career/retirement life; completed the Toolkit Worksheets; and developed your Retirement Survival Action Plan, you should now take the final step and declare your intention to follow through.

As you proceed with your retirement life planning, be certain you always consider and honor your answers to these questions. As you move into your retirement life, you will want to revisit these questions and adjust your plans appropriately. If you make the effort to base your decisions on the values clarification and visualizations you have done, periodically answer the three life questions and update your Action Plan you are more likely to live a "successful" retirement life filled with meaning and joy.

AND ALWAYS REMEMBER:

- LIVE YOUR RETIREMENT LIFE ON PURPOSE NOT BY "DEFAULT."

- ADOPT A POSITIVE ATTITUDE.

- REDEFINE "SUCCESS" IN RETIREMENT.
- ACKNOWLEDGE YOUR NEWFOUND POWER AND FREEDOM.
- DO SOMETHING WONDERFUL!

PART FIVE

Our Legacy And Challenge
What We've Learned,
How to Share It, and
Why We Must!

With all due respect to the Founding Mothers of the Feminist Movement, the sea tide of change in societal norms has brought to the surface a veritable island of kelp torn loose from the ocean floor leaving a swarm of sand flies in their wake. Those annoying attitudinal remnants from the past persist long after every historic period fades and irrespective of how many tides rush in and out. They return relentlessly in waves of denial of the strides that were made on our behalf. "We-Who-Are-All-Knowing" shake our graying heads, just as the generation who preceded us must have done, as we observe the Millennials and Gen Xs taking for granted (or ignoring) paths that were carved out for them a lifetime ago. They have only the slightest inkling of what it meant to "hit the glass ceiling"; to be a "token" woman in law school, medical school or engineering college; or on the most fundamental level, to dream of a career beyond the little house with the white picket fence. Forget about not having the right to vote! Even we have difficulty internalizing the pre-Suffragette era.

We're not blaming the offspring of today's "Wikipedia" generation for their lack of appreciation or understanding about how profoundly women's aspirational lives were altered by what happened in the 1960s. But like generations before us, and those who follow us, we don't want it to go unnoticed. We sadly observe glimpses, that we fear are signs of our power eroding: fewer young women participating in women's rights organizations; rampant exploitation of the female body in internet/ social network posts; what seems to us to be a laissez-faire attitude about planning for the future. Now we're really sounding like "old farts"! But we think with the surface-to-air missiles of superficial information that bombard all of us, and that may lack both depth and precision, we can, and should be responsible for more than cursory and impersonal "sound bites" when it comes to the future for women born in the New Millennium.

It's not that we don't trust the young women who were born after us to make a difference for the better, they certainly have the ability, drive and intelligence to make significant contributions to our society. It's just that we Boomers have a pattern of blazing trails, creating new paths or just seeing new options, and then going for it. We marched to the beat of a different drummer during the sexual revolution, in opposition to a war, in both foreign countries and in the business environment of our own country. As young women we took the risks, probably without the awareness we were even taking a risk. Now we're at a different transitional stage where taking risks may be a choice of necessity and judging from the women we interviewed and the messages we are reading on many of the blog sites associated with this generation, we're ready to take some new risks.

Our "legacy" if you will, can be as complex or simple as we choose. The important thing is to find a mechanism that works for each of us to share what we've learned. Here are some suggested guidelines for telling our own stories, and how to go about it.

TELLING YOUR OWN STORY

"A life unexamined is not a Life worth Living"- Socrates

EVERYBODY HAS A STORY AND THIS IS YOURS!

Each of us is unique and by the time we are ready to retire, we have a very interesting and powerful life story to be told. You don't have to be a celebrity, a politician or a rock star to tell your story. You don't have to prepare it for publication or distribution, but rather as an additional exercise in the process of reviewing and honoring your own unique life experiences. Perhaps one day you may share your story with your children or grandchildren as your "legacy" or inheritance to them. According to the Merriam Webster Dictionary, one definition of the word legacy is "something that is or may be inherited." Therefore, your life story (or memoir) qualifies as your legacy.

It is important to begin your story in early childhood. According to Dr. Morris Massey in his work, "What You Are Is What You Were When," we are "value- programmed" at a time when we are young and impressionable, (usually between the ages of 9 and 18). The stories told to us, and our early experiences and relationships, affect our attitudes and understanding of the world and ourselves. This is when our values, ethics, morals, behavior and sense of self are formed. When we examine these early experiences and influences, we gain valuable insight and understanding into our own story. Although some of our core values do change as we experience life and test them out ourselves, many remain with us our entire lives.

POSSIBLE TOPICS FOR YOUR STORY INCLUDE:

- What are your early childhood memories? How did these events impact you?

- What were your early interests? Have you followed these interests? How have your interests changed?

- Who were your family members and what are their memorable traits? How have your family members influenced your values, behavior and sense of self?

- Who were your best friends growing up? Why were you attracted to each?

- What were your favorite games, toys, books, movies as you were growing up? What interested you about these?

- Who were your favorite teachers? Why?

- Who were your early role models? What did you learn from them?

- What was the political, social and economic situation during your value-programming period? How did (does) that affect your current perspective? (An entertaining historical book about "The Boomer Century 1946-2046" by Richard Crocker, is a good resource).

- What social and technological changes have you seen in your lifetime?

- List Your Defining Moments (i.e. situations that profoundly impacted you, have changed your outlook, or taught you an important life lesson).

- Describe your education history. How has this influenced your life?

- Describe your career decisions. Why did you make these decisions? How has this influenced your life?

- Explain the important life choices that you made. Why did you make them? How would you evaluate them?

- What accomplishment(s) are you most proud of? Why?

- What words do others use to describe you? Why?

- What words would you use to describe yourself? Why?

- What are your favorite words? Why?

- What are your favorite books and movies as an adult? Why?

- What would you consider your "Pearls of Wisdom" or life lessons learned for others?

- Do you have any unfinished business to attend to? (i.e. a relationship to mend, a wrong to right, a road not taken, dreams not manifested).

- Additional Information Optional.

Review all your information and begin to celebrate your unique story and your life!

This exercise can be very cathartic for you, and the results, if you decide to share them, can be a priceless gift to those you know and care about.

Following are some tips for beginning this exercise:

1. Decide on and establish a deadline in order to avoid the "procrastination pitfall."

2. Create your own "sacred space" for writing by surrounding yourself with treasured items (a rock from a favorite hike, a picture, a special memento, music, flowers).

3. Determine how you will write this: electronically -- computer-generated and saved to a CD; PowerPoint with photos and scanned items; series of iMovies; podcasts; Skype videos; or handwritten in a leather bound journal, a school tablet, or your favorite letter paper. If you already have a life journal, decide how will you categorize or index this? Perhaps this will prompt you to actually write a memoir in the near future.

4. Plan to whom and how you will pass it along.

The authors feel that your life story document is very important to future generations of women and others and not just for genetic clarity. In this age of technology and instant gratification, perhaps this will provide your readers with a very absent sense of place and self in a somewhat rootless society that exists today. All of us wish we knew more than the tiny fragments of information we have about our own histories and those that came before us. We may have no real sense of who our ancestors were as individuals -- their hopes and dreams, their challenges and sufferings, and the lessons they could have taught us if we knew them.

The following section includes further resources to assist you in expanding your knowledge and awareness of how to do more than survive and to successfully transition to this important and wonderful stage of life.

The best of luck to you -- and to us all!

PART SIX

THE EMPTY DESK SURVIVAL GUIDE RESOURCES

BOOKS:

- *Age Power-How the 21st Century Will Be Ruled by the New Old*, and *The Power Years -A User's Guide to the Rest of Your Life,* and *With Purpose: Going from Success to Significance in Work and Life* - Ken Dychtwald

- *A Baby Boomers Journey to Middle Age* - Beverly Mahone

- *A Fresh Map of Life: The Emergence of the Third Age* - Peter Lasiett

- *Baby Boomer Retirement- 65 Simple Ways to Protect Your Future* - Don Silver

- *The Best Home Businesses for People 50 Plus-Opportunities for People Who Believe the Best is Yet to Be* - Paul and Sarah Edwards

- *The Breaking Point: How Today's Women Are Navigating The Midlife Crisis* - Sue Shellenbarger

- *Boomer Preneurs: How Baby Boomers Can Start Their Own Business, Make Money and Enjoy Life* - Mary Beth Izard

- *Doing Sixty & Seventy* - Gloria Steinem

- *Feel the Fear and Do It Anyway* - Susan Jeffers

- *Has Anyone Seen My Reading Glasses? The Humorous and Slightly Informative Chronicles of a Retired Baby Boomer* - Pat Paciello

- *How to Love Your Retirement* - Barbara Waxman and Robert A. Mendelson

- *How to Retire, Happy, Wild and Free: Retirement Wisdom That You Won't Get From Your Financial Advisor,* and *The Joy of Not Working: A Book for the Retired, Unemployed and Overworked* - Ernie Zellinski

- *Live Long Live Rich- Creating Your Retirement Paycheck* - H. Craig Rappaport

- *Prime Time-How Baby Boomers Will Revolutionize Retirement and Transform America,* and *The Big Shift: Navigating the New Stage Beyond Midlife* - Marc Freedman

- *Reinventing Myself: Memoirs of a Retired Professor* - Marlys Marshal Stynne

- *Rethinking Retirement-How to Create the Life You Want Without Waiting to Retire* - Keith J. Weber

- *The Right Questions* - Debbie Ford

- *Second Acts* - Stephen M. Pollan and Mark Levine

- *Second Careers- New Ways to Work After 50* - Caroline Bird

- *The Seven Spiritual Laws of Yoga* - Deepak Chopra and David Simon

- *The Soul of Money: Reclaiming the Wealth of Our Inner Resources* - Teresa Barker

- *What Color is Your Parachute? For Retirement: Planning Now for the Life You Want* - John E. Nelson

- *What's Next? Follow Your Passion and Find Your Dream Job* - Kerry Hannon

- *What You Are Is What You Were When...Again* (DVD) - Morris Massey

- *When Baby Boomer Women Retire* - Nancy Dailey

- *Who Moved My Cheese?* - Spencer Johnson

WEBSITES:
Information
American Association of Retired Persons (AARP) www.aarp.org; www.aarp.org/families/caregiving; volunteers.aarp.org
Baby Boomer Women's Journal-Study www.genpolicy.com/freecopy/index.html
Caregiving
THE CAREGIVING BOOM: BABY BOOMER WOMEN GIVING CARE-Survey: www.caregiving.org/data/archives/babyboomer.pdf
Disability Travel - www.disabilitytravel.com
Financial - www.smartmoney.com
Government
    Internal Revenue Service (IRS) - www.irs.gov
    Social Security Administration - www.ssa.gov
Health and Age - www.healthandage.com
International Council on Active Aging - www.icaa.cc
Retirement Planning
    www.baby-boomers-planning-for-retirement.com

www.bestretirementplanningresources.com

www.gotoretirement.com

www.lifeafterfulltimework.com

www.retirementplanninghandbook.com

www.creativeretirementcoach@gmail.com

(Arlene Chemers: creativeretirementcoach@gmail.com)

www.humanresourceinvestments.com

(Barbara Bannon: hri@cox.net)

Senior Net - www.seniornet.org

Seniors Travel Guide - www.seniorstravelguide.com

Too Young to Retire - www.2young2retire.com

Vacation Home Exchange - www.independentliving.org/vacaswap.
html

Assessment

www.discovering what's next.com

www.encore.org/marcfreedman

Strong Interest Inventory – www.cpp.com

www.onetcenter.org/tools.html

Road to Resilience Values Deck: (card exercise to discover your
values)

www.roadtoresilience.com; www.amazon.com

Volunteering

Elderhostel – www.elderhostel.org

Elder Treks - www.eldertreks.com

Executive Service Corps – www.escus.org

www.volunteermatch.org

www.experiencecorps.org/

www.nationalservice.gov/questions/app/ask

Habitat for Humanity – www.habitat.org

Peace Corps - www.peacecorps.gov/index.cfm

Score (SBA) - www.score.org

www.volunteersexpeditions.org

BLOGS/FORUMS

Womenontheverge---ofretirement.blogspot.com
www.internsover40.blogspot.com
www.havefundogood.blogspot.com
www.aboomerslifeafter50.blogspot.com
www.boomerwomenspeak.com/forum
www.nabbw.com/
www.ayearto50.blogspot.com/

FOR COACHING, PRESENTATIONS AND WORKSHOPS BASED ON "THE EMPTY DESK SURVIAL GUIDE" PLEASE CONTACT US AT:

creativeretirementcoach@gmail.com or hri@cox.net.

VISIT US AT OUR BLOG:

Womenontheverge-ofretirement.blogspot.com

ABOUT THE AUTHORS:

BARBARA BANNON: As an Organizational consultant and coach, Barbara Bannon has spoken and/or consulted with over 500,000 people in Corporate America in her 25+ year career. Her last corporate position was with a Fortune 500 company where she was responsible for employee relations, recruiting and hiring for 900 Headquarters employees, and training and organization development corporate-wide for @6000 employees. She has been the principal consultant of Human Resource Investments for 20 years.

Barbara's areas of focus have been: conflict resolution and mediation, she is a certified mediator through the Supreme Court of Oklahoma, performance management, executive and management coaching, teambuilding, interviewing and selection, customer service, workplace diversity, meeting management, organizational assessment and planning, and consulting skills.

Barbara's client coaching experiences vary from working with technical executives with engineering backgrounds as well as medical executives to petroleum industry managers. The level of responsibility with which she has focused in these organizations vary from first line supervisors to top team executives. A few of the companies who have used her coaching services are: Newfield Petroleum, American Airlines, Pryer Machine, Matrix AEP, Arinc, Dollar Thrifty Car Rental and Dean Foods.

In 2005 she was awarded the Paragon Award from Leadership Tulsa for outstanding community leadership. Additionally, she received the award for Outstanding Contributor in Training and

Development from The Tulsa Area ASTD chapter and has been nominated three times by her clients as an "Outstanding Contributor in Human Resources." As an adjunct professor in the Spears School of Business at Oklahoma State University, Barbara has also been recognized as an outstanding professor.

She has authored many articles and her most recent publication is a book entitled "Risky Business, Overcoming Fear and Mastering the Art of Conflict Resolution."

ARLENE CHEMERS: Arlene Chemers is a Certified Retirement Coach and Professional Coach. Arlene Chemers' extensive experience in career development, training, counseling and coaching in the corporate, management consulting and outplacement arenas makes her highly-qualified to make a strong contribution to "The Empty Desk Survival Guide". She was formerly associated with an international outplacement firm and VP of a management consulting firm providing executive coaching and outplacement. She served as Corporate Manager of Employee Development for a Fortune 500 corporation.

Her background also includes authoring and conducting Career Development and Job Search Skill training programs, Executive and Management Coaching, Career and Professional Coaching, Retirement Coaching and Transition Management.

In addition to holding a Masters Degree in Human Resource Management from the University of Utah where she specialized in Career Development, Training and Organizational Development, she is a Certified Professional Coach, and holds certificates as a Life-Time Senior Professional in Human Resources (SPHR) as a Career Management Professional (CMP) and is a Certified Retirement Options Coach.

An active leader in a variety of prestigious professional associations and community service boards, Arlene is currently a member of the International Coach Federation, and has been president of the American Society for Training and Development (ASTD) in Salt Lake City, Utah; VP of the Tulsa Area ASTD, and served on the Board of Business in Training Services for Tulsa Technology Center, the Education Workgroup for the American Petroleum Institute, Tulsa Consumer Credit Counseling Center and is a founding member of the Cancer Wellness House in Salt Lake.

Arlene is passionate in her commitment to helping people make meaningful career and life decisions and successful transitions that will lead to lives filled with satisfaction and purpose, at any stage of life.

MARYLOVE THRALLS: Marylove Thralls holds a Masters Degree in Human Relations (MHR) from the University of Oklahoma and is an accredited public relations professional who has worked extensively with both corporate and non-profit organizations. She has been a public relations consultant and fundraising event planner. While serving on the management team of an international manufacturing organization, she was responsible for diversity training, quality assurance training programs, employee relations activities and corporate communications. She has served as Director of Development and Director of Marketing for several non-profit organizations both in Oklahoma and California. She has written professional journal articles in the human relations field and has two published novels, "Kiss the Son" and "Grace Notes." She currently works as a public relations consultant and teaches marketing and communications at Santa Barbara City College.

Throughout her career Marylove has served on boards of directors and as a consultant to a wide range of agencies that address women's issues, provide services to victims of domestic abuse, the developmentally disabled and the homeless, as well as many performing arts organizations.

Made in the USA
Charleston, SC
14 June 2012